Exploring the Little Rivers
of New Jersey

JAMES and MARGARET CAWLEY

Exploring the Little Rivers

of New Jersey

RUTGERS UNIVERSITY PRESS
New Brunswick, New Jersey

Other books by James and Margaret Cawley

Along the Old York Road
Along the Delaware and Raritan Canal

By James Cawley

Historic New Jersey in Pictures

Maps by Frank Kelland

Affectionately dedicated to our daughters,
Margaret Elizabeth Cawley,
Jeanne C. Marshall,
and Nancy C. Jerome

Contents

Preface

Canoeing, which was the earliest means of transportation in this hemisphere (after walking), is now one of the fastest growing forms of recreation. In 1969 *a quarter of a million new canoes* were purchased in the United States.

With modern aluminum and plastic craft, fitted with air chambers or other flotation devices, one may safely use a canoe in any kind of water except the open ocean. However, the most enjoyable kind of canoeing, in the opinion of the authors, is on some little stream with sufficient depth to enable the cruiser to follow it in a canoe without too much wading, and where it is constantly a mystery as to what is around the next bend. As one writer expressed it, ". . . a river is the coziest of friends; you must love it and live with it before you know it."

The authors believe that the little rivers of New Jersey offer more enjoyment for those who may want to paddle for an afternoon, a day, or even longer, than does any other area. They vary from rivers like the Raritan, flowing through open meadows, to the wilder streams of the Wharton State Forest in the Pine Barrens of New Jersey.

Since the publication of our first book about the rivers of New Jersey in 1942, some physical changes have occurred on the streams. Some dams have been washed out, trees blown down across the rivers and there have been other regular happenings in nature. During the past year we have re-explored every river described in this edition and the Delaware and Raritan Canal and feeder, and we found surprisingly little change in the conditions on the streams. In a few of our rivers there is noticeable pollution but many of them seem still clean. Perhaps the current efforts to restore our environment will save our little rivers from further spoilage before it is too late. In our growing concern about such matters we are reminded of the words in Milton's *Paradise Lost:*

> Accuse not Nature:
> She hath done her part;
> Do thou but thine.

For the greater enjoyment of those who may follow our trails we recommend the use of the growing number of state and county parks that are on or near many of the rivers covered in this volume. Most of them offer such facilities as swimming, picnicking, and camping. In some cases, at a reasonable cost, comfortable overnight cabins and lean-tos are available for those who may not care to camp along the streams.

One noticeable change we observed, as we rechecked the rivers last year, was that camp sites formerly available on private land were not open to canoeists without specific permission from the owners of the land. In many cases the landowners are hard to find, but the additional state and county parks, with more adequate facilities, have solved that problem in most situations.

We have included in this edition a list of canoe rentals,

a suggested reading list of books about the countryside through which the rivers flow, and a new feature in description and photographs of the equipment we use.

If a canoe is rented from a place like Ben's, on the Rancocas, or from the Winding River Campground on the Great Egg Harbor River, for example, ask the proprietor about the conditions on the rivers. Better still, using the maps at the beginning of the chapters in this book and the oil company highway maps, explore the stream of your choice by car before cruising it in a canoe. Such exploration will insure a more enjoyable canoe journey and what is more important, acquaint the canoeist with the hazards, if any, that are likely to be encountered.

Happy Days Afloat!

THE AUTHORS

October 1970

Exploring the Little Rivers
of New Jersey

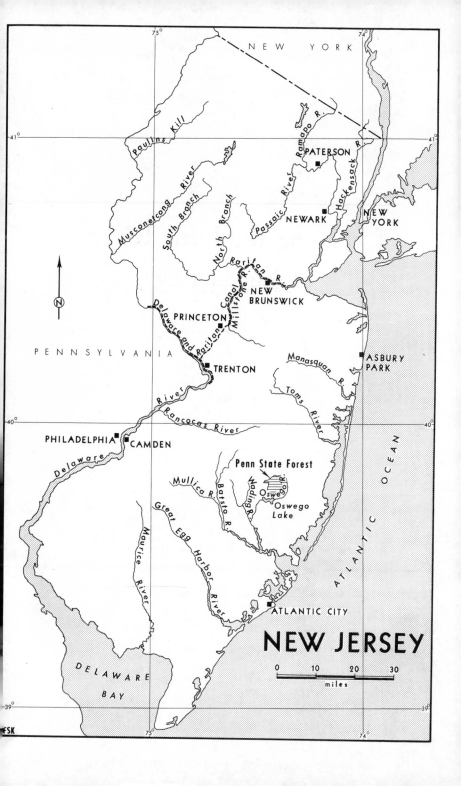

NEW YORK

PATERSON

Ramapo R.

Paulins Kill

Musconetcong River

South Branch

North Branch

Passaic River

Hackensack R.

NEWARK

NEW YORK

N

Raritan

Raritan R.

NEW BRUNSWICK

Canal

Millstone R.

Delaware and Raritan

PRINCETON

PENNSYLVANIA

Manasquan R.

ASBURY PARK

TRENTON

River

Toms River

Rancocas River

PHILADELPHIA CAMDEN

Delaware

Penn State Forest

Mullica R.

Batsto R.

Wading R.

Oswego R.

Oswego Lake

ATLANTIC OCEAN

Great Egg Harbor River

Maurice River

ATLANTIC CITY

NEW JERSEY

0   10   20   30
miles

DELAWARE BAY

FSK

Re-exploring the Little Waterways

Anyone familiar with the wilderness areas of the canoe country in northern Minnesota or Canada might believe the photograph above was taken in such a place. It would be a natural assumption, but actually the scene is the Wading River, in the New Jersey Pine Barrens, where such beautiful skylines of the white cedar are commonplace. Throughout the Wharton State Forest and other areas of the Barrens there are several rivers with equally entrancing views. On many of the streams, as one quietly glides down the usually fast-moving amber cedar water, it doesn't seem possible that one can return to the metropolitan centers within an hour by car. The New Jersey Turnpike and the Garden State Parkway carry the country's busiest traffic on the edges of the unique and mysterious land of the Pine Barrens.

More and more people are beginning to realize that readily accessible to the entire metropolitan areas of Philadelphia and New York there is a world of adventure, recreation, and natural loveliness in New Jersey. It is easy to reach by car or public transportation. One may explore this charming countryside by car, or better still, quietly paddling a canoe down any one of the many little rivers of the state. Exploring by canoe enables one not only to savor the smell of the pines and cedars and observe the wildlife along the streams, but also to get to know the rivers in a way not possible otherwise. Robert Louis Stevenson expressed it this way:

There is no music like a little river's. It plays the same tune (and that's the favourite) over and over again, and yet does not weary of it like men fiddlers. It takes the mind out-of-doors; and, though we should be grateful for good houses, there is, after all, no house like God's out-of-doors.

And, we may add, a little river helps one to cultivate a sense of inner quietude, so needed today.

To be able to launch a canoe in a river, where conditions are sometimes truly wild in every sense of the word, where mile after mile, the stately white cedars surround the canoeist with beauty, with the fast, foam-flecked water rushing around the bend, makes such a day on a river a rare adventure. Remnants of forgotten towns from the early days of the Iron Empire and the many species of rare wild plants that may be found, all are a part of a land area in the South Jersey country comprising one quarter of the total land area of the State. We have been told that if one knows where to look it is not difficult, even today, to find an operating still in some of the remote places in the Barrens. It was the land of the smuggler and privateer

4

during the American Revolution and, during the early years, law enforcement officers found it better not to venture too far into some of those remote areas.

Not all the rivers are as wild, of course, yet even those like the North or South Branch of the Raritan, the Millstone, and others in more settled country have a charm of their own. The quiet countryside, the cattle peacefully grazing in the meadows beside the streams, the well-kept farms, provide a different but equally rewarding experience.

Now that camp sites are available in the parks and along the towpath of the Delaware and Raritan Canal, plan to spend a night or more camping during cruises. If wood is available for an evening campfire, the tantalizing smell of the wood smoke will be an additional pleasure.

The inexperienced canoeist should not at first attempt to navigate the wilder rivers in South Jersey. Begin by taking your own or renting a canoe for a few hours' practice on such waters as the Delaware and Raritan Canal or on the canal feeder where there are no snags to turn the canoe over. Of course this should not be attempted by non-swimmers. As for learning to handle a paddle, the Boy Scout merit badge pamphlet on canoeing is the best guide we know.

A familiar sight on most highways these days is a passing car or an eight-canoe trailer loaded with canoes. It was not too long ago that to see even one car with a canoe on its top was a rare sight, even in New Jersey with its profusion of canoeing waters.

For those who may be inspired by this book to try a real cruise, we suggest that one of our little rivers be selected; then before your actual trip, carefully explore by car that part of the stream of the intended journey, viewing the river from as many bridges and other vantage points as possible. Knowing the condition of the waters, places where a canoe may have to be carried, will make a more enjoyable and easier canoe cruise. On such exploratory trips one can determine the best way to get to the starting point and the best place to get by road from the end of the journey to the car that had been left at the start.

Such little problems as how best to carry around a mill dam or over or around a fallen tree, getting wet from a capsized canoe or a sudden shower, are to be expected and once you get accustomed to them they are easily accepted as part of the adventure.

Carry along bird and flower guidebooks and you will be surprised at the wildlife that may be seen along New Jersey's little waterways. In some places, such as the Pine Barrens, will be found many species of plant life seldom seen anywhere else.

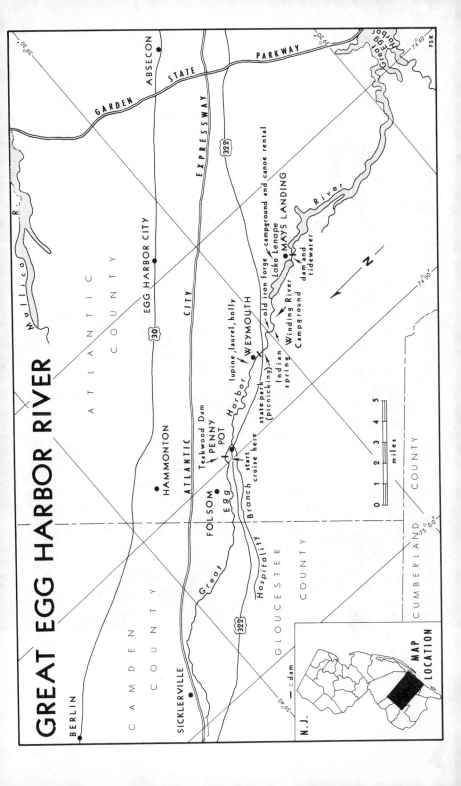

GREAT EGG HARBOR RIVER

The small beginning of the Great Egg Harbor River near its source below Berlin. From this point to Penny Pot the river is too difficult for comfortable canoe cruising

The Great Egg Harbor River

Route 30, from Atlantic City to Camden, practically parallels the course of the Great Egg Harbor River. It affords a convenient road by which the traveler may view this stream and also provides easy access for starting canoe trips.

The source of the stream is a small pond near Berlin in Camden County, and it is not much more than a brook until the Penny Pot and the Hospitality branches add their flow to the main stream at Sicklerville. It is possible to cruise on the Hospitality branch, but it is a very wild, tangled stream and tough going all the way. We would not recommend it to our readers.

Near the little hamlet of Penny Pot, where the river passes under Route 322, the wild beauty of the stream becomes evident. In season it is a riot of laurel, lupine, holly, and other plant life native to this section of the country. It is at this point that most canoe parties embark for the journey to Mays Landing.

Route 322, or the Black Horse Pike as it is better known, is an express highway and cars may not be parked on the shoulders. For canoeists starting a cruise at Penny Pot we suggest that permission be asked to park cars in the lot of the Snack Bar, east of the road. Their parking facilities are for customers, so a cup of coffee and perhaps a hamburger would be in order while requesting permission to park.

It is possible to launch canoes below the dam but a better place is about one hundred feet downriver that can be

Co-author Jim Cawley enjoying a workout with a single blade in the swift water at the Winding River Camp Ground landing, above Mays Landing

reached by a sand driveway. The land is posted, however, and permission should be asked before using that launching place.

Last May, during a cruise from Penny Pot to Mays Landing, we discovered a new facility that will, in our opinion, make any one day or weekend cruise on the Great Egg Harbor more enjoyable and solve the problem of how to get car drivers back to Penny Pot at the end of the trip. It it called The Winding River Camp Ground. At the invitation of the owners, Mr. and Mrs. Al Horsey, we inspected their delightfully wooded campground, on a high bluff above the river. We were very much impressed, not only with this better than usually maintained facility but also with the courtesy and willingness of the owners to help canoeists in any way they can.

In the past, cruisers either had to end their trips at Weymouth, where it is possible to get out of the river, or continue all the way to Mays Landing. For those who may still wish to do that, the place to end the trip is at the Lenape Amusement Park. However, for many a better plan would be to stop at the Winding River Camp ground a few miles above Mays Landing and arrange to have Mr. Horsey drive you back to your car at Penny Pot.

On a weekend canoe trip from Sicklerville to Mays Landing we retraced a route described by Henry Van Dyke in a story, "Between the Lupin and the Laurel," published in 1907. Van Dyke wrote of canoeing with four Quaker companions down a "mysterious" South Jersey river, the name of which he did not disclose, as he believed "that the name of the hiding-place should not be published, lest the careless, fad-following crowd should flock thither and spoil it." We do not feel as Van Dyke did about such things— they should be shared and enjoyed by all, and we quote a part of his description of the river, which is still very much as it was when Van Dyke "discovered" it:

It was thus that my four friends—Friends in creed as well as in deed—told me . . . of their secret find of a little river in South Jersey, less than an hour from Philadelphia, where one could float in a canoe through mile after mile of unbroken woodland, and camp at night in a bit of wilderness as wildly fair as when the wigwams of the Lenni-Lenape were hidden among its pine groves. The Friends said they "had a concern" to guide me to their delectable retreat and they hoped "the way would open" for me to come. . . .

Our "earthly labor" began again when we started down the stream; for now we had fairly entered the long strip of wilderness which curtains its winding course. On either hand the thickets came down so close to the water that there were no banks left; just woods and water blending; and the dark topaz current swirling and gurgling through a clump of bushes or round the trunk of a tree, as if it did not care what path it took, so long as it got through. Adlers and pussy-willows, viburnums, clethras, choke-cherries, swamp maples, red birches, and all sorts of trees and shrubs that are water loving, made an intricate labyrinth for the stream to thread; and through the tangle, cat-briers, blackberries, fox grapes, and poison ivy were interlaced. . . .

It was no easy task to guide the boat down the swift current, for it was bewilderingly crooked, twisting and turning upon itself in a way that would make the fair Meander look like a straight line. . . .

How charming was the curve of that brown, foam-flecked stream, as it rushed swiftly down, from pool to pool, under the ancient, over-hanging elms, willows and sycamores.

In 1935, as we were doing the research and photography for our first book about the little rivers of New Jersey, we set out to locate Van Dyke's "mysterious" river. We finally discovered it, despite the fact that he had made it difficult by using such names as "Hummington" for Hammonton and "Watermouth" for Weymouth. Van Dyke had been cruising the Great Egg Harbor River.

It was a lovely May day when we loaded our little fifteen-foot, forty-five pound canoe on the top of our station wagon to follow the route of Van Dyke and his Quaker companions. It was apparent that we were not going to be able to paddle near the source of the river. We did manage to follow it by car and at Penny Pot launch the canoe for the start of the cruise. At this point the river was narrow with swift-flowing water. Overhead the foliage formed a green arch. Occasionally we had to carry over or around fallen trees.

The many cranberry bogs in this vicinity reminded us that our traditional feast of turkey and cranberries was passed along to the white man by the Indians, according to legend. Whether that is so or not, it is a fact that this region was plentifully supplied with wild cranberries and turkeys at one time. The wild cranberries may still be found in abundance.

The hand-crafted scoop with which all cranberries were harvested until machines came into use. It is still used in some smaller bogs

It was not until the early part of the nineteenth century that cranberries were grown for the market. Cape Cod was the place where this fruit was first cultivated on a large scale for the market and it is the largest cranberry-growing area in the country today.

The wild and swampy areas of the upper part of the Great Egg Harbor River are ideal for the cultivation of cranberries, and it is the principal money crop of this region. From December to April the bogs are flooded to protect the vines from frost, and in the spring the water is drawn off. In early summer the berries begin to show and by harvest time they are very colorful. During the harvesting season, in September, the bogs are a hive of activity and are filled with the pickers.

During one of our trips of river exploration that summer, as we were launching our canoe for a cruise down the Great

This crude dam, built to flood a cranberry bog, is unique in that the teak-wood timbers used in its construction were salvaged from eighteenth-century American battleships

Egg Harbor River, we met the owner of the adjoining land, Mr. John Kinney, who expressed great interest in our trip. When he learned that we were gathering material for a book he gave us some new information about the locality. "This place," remarked Mr. Kinney, "is known as Penny Pot, and it was so named in 1686 by the first settlers because it resembled the countryside of their native home in England."

We inquired about the purpose of the dam and were told that it was originally used as a cranberry dam and later to furnish power for a gristmill. An unusual fact about the dam is the material of which it is made. The cost of lumber for such a dam would ordinarily be about $600, but this one has timber in it that had at that time a market value of about $75,000. It seems a friend of Mr. Kinney sent him truckloads of teak timber, salvaged from old warships, when he heard he needed lumber for a new dam. It is doubtless the only dam in the country built of that costly wood.

Five minutes after leaving the dam the river became a wilderness; trees crowding the stream, in places actually shutting out all sunlight; the shores a profusion of lupine, holly, and laurel. The pine trees and a combination of white sand and clay along the shores were in vivid contrast to the foliage overhead. The journey from Penny Pot to Weymouth was one of endless beauty, without many signs of civilization along the way. It seems incredible that such wilderness may be found within thirty miles of Philadelphia. Such conditions are not unusual in the 750,000 acres known as the Pine Barrens.

Today many more signs of civilization are evident, but it is remarkable that so few buildings or other evidences of the population explosion are to be seen between Penny Pot and Weymouth.

It is not possible for the motorist to get to the river at many points between Penny Pot and Weymouth, but the general character of the river may be seen above and below Weymouth.

This village is worth a thorough inspection. The places of interest and the colorful history of this onetime thriving community are fascinating. The visitor will find a tangle of vine-covered ruins that were once the scene of industrial activity. Under the ruins of the paper mill in the state park on the river at Weymouth stood the Weymouth Iron Works, built in 1801. The extensive land holdings of the Weymouth Company of iron bogs, timber lands for charcoal, worker housing, and other facilities necessary for such an operation made this one of the largest of its kind in the Pine Barrens. During the War of 1812 grapeshot and cannon balls were produced in this forge for the U.S. Navy.

The ore was bog iron from local pits, and in smelting it eight wagonloads of charcoal were used for a single charge of the furnace. It was crude but effective, and from such simple beginnings came our present-day complicated steel industry. Not far from the furnace one may find the remains of the roadbed that was once a mule-power railroad, used to haul products to Mays Landing.

Nearby is the famous Indian Spring, which has flowed steadily through wet and dry seasons for centuries. It is still the source of drinking water for people of the vicinity. On a high bank overlooking the river formerly stood the old manor house which was built in the eighteenth century. Its entire frame was of local cedar.

Sometimes the river, particularly from Penny Pot to Weymouth, may be a bit difficult to run due to fallen trees, etc. If the upper reaches of the stream below Weymouth are shallow, as they sometimes are in the summer, the cruise can be ended at Weymouth where it is easy to get out of the river and to the road. However, this should be decided before starting downriver as a car should be left at Weymouth for transportation back to the other cars left at Penny Pot. Your options in the event that the river is too low or clogged below Weymouth would be to carry the canoe on your car down to Mays Landing and spend more time on the lower, Lake Lenape, part of the stream or call it a day and run the lower section on another day.

For those who may prefer to spend a day paddling or sailing on Lake Lenape, which is that part of the river from the dam at Mays Landing upstream for a mile or so, we suggest launching your canoe at the public beach or, if a canoe is rented, start your day at Lenape Amusement Park a bit upstream from the public beach. A day on the lake, when there is not too much wind, is delightful.

All that remains of an early paper mill that was built on the foundations of the eighteenth-century Weymouth Iron Works

IN
MEMORY OF
ROSANA IRELAND
BABINGTON
who departed this life
JULY 13th 1825
Aged 18 Months
O death it was a x... call
A sudden judgement to us all

In the churchyard at Weymouth are several of the unusual iron grave markers, cast at the nearby Weymouth Iron Works. This one is nearly 150 years old, and being pure cast iron, it may last for several hundred more years

Along the shore of Lake Lenape from the public beach at Mays Landing.
This water is the impounded lower reaches of the fresh-water Great Egg
Harbor River and is the scene of a great deal of boating activity

For bird lovers, poking in and out of the many bays along the shores will be rewarding. All kinds of marsh birds are found and in fact you may be lucky, as we have frequently been, to spot an osprey.

In late May the entire river is a scene of unsurpassed beauty. Miles of blossoming laurel with a background of stately pines unfold before the canoeist as he travels along. On a quiet day the entire scene is duplicated in shadow form beneath the canoe.

About halfway to Mays Landing the river widens out with large areas of backwaters on either shore, offering endless opportunities for exploration. The river bottom is of pure white sand, delightful to walk upon in your bare feet. Deer and other game are plentiful.

Jeanne Cawley Marshall, daughter of the authors, canoeing on Lake Carnegie

The Millstone

Mattawong was the Indian name for this river and it meant "hard to travel." Conditions must have changed considerably since the early days, as we know of no other stream that is so placid and so easy to negotiate.

Like so many of the smaller streams of the state, the Millstone has its source in a swamp or small woodland pond. One branch is the outlet of a swampy pond near Manalapin on Route 33; the other starts near Hightstown, not far away.

Winding their tortuous ways through swampland and woods and at times twisting back upon the original course in long, sluggish loops, the two branches meet a few miles east of Princeton. A riot of vegetation lines the shores for miles and the very nature of the country provides a perfect bird sanctuary. Wild ducks, bittern, heron, and many other species may be found in abundance. The color of the autumn leaves along the Millstone is marvelous to see.

From the junction of the two branches to Route 1 is only a few miles and it is below the road a short distance, where the river passes under the canal, that the canoeists should start their trip downriver. It is a simple matter to provide oneself with the transportation facilities for a canoe journey of a few hours, a day—or even a weekend, if the objective is to cruise the entire river.

Passing under the one hundred and thirty-seven-year-old Delaware and Raritan Canal, which is carried over the river by an aqueduct, the river then becomes Lake Carnegie. The

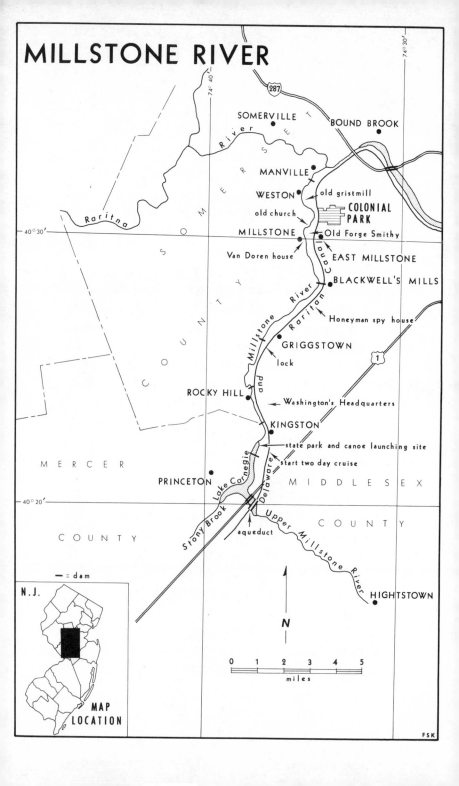

The canoe house on the west shore of Lake Carnegie as it appeared before its removal several years ago. Canoeing groups from as far away as Maryland regularly began their spring cruises here

canoeist will of course have to carry up and over the canal and into Lake Carnegie at this point. The generosity of the late Andrew Carnegie made possible this delightful man-made lake, which not only adds to the beauty of the countryside but also provides a place for rowing, canoeing, and other aquatic sports for Princeton University and the community of Princeton. It was built in 1906 through the simple expedient of constructing a dam across a natural valley between the highway and the Delaware and Raritan Canal. The lake is about three miles long and perhaps a quarter of a mile wide, flanked on the east by the canal towpath and on the west by the winding wooded shores on the outskirts of Princeton. At the upper end of the lake stands the commodious boathouse in which the shells of the University are kept. Such famed events as the Childs Cup Race are

This venerable weeping willow was grown from a branch of a tree that grew near the grave of Napoleon on St. Helena. The building is the Princeton University boathouse on Lake Carnegie

A Sunday club race of sunfish class boats on Lake Carnegie

The Cornell University crew rigging their shells in preparation for a
spring race on Lake Carnegie

25

held on the lake in the spring. During recent years the popularity of dinghy racing has come to Princeton and there is now quite a large fleet of sailing dinghies moored near the lower end where the lake is wider and the breezes steadier. When cold weather comes Lake Carnegie is popular with the skaters and skate sailors who may be seen skimming over its smooth surface during the winter weekends.

Stony Brook empties into the south end of the lake and helps to provide a constant supply of water. All the land along the west shore of Lake Carnegie is privately owned and picnicking is not allowed. However, across the lake anywhere on the canal towpath picknicking is permitted but cars are not allowed on this or any other part of the towpath.

Below the dam on Lake Carnegie the river again assumes its natural form and this part of the stream to the mill dam, a hundred yards below, is good bass fishing water. It is here also that a great variety of bird life may be seen, including a flock of Canadian geese during the fall and spring months. It is a great thrill to hear them honking and to see them swinging down in the typical large flying "V."

The Millstone River is interesting not only from a scenic point of view but in many other respects. According to geologists, it flowed in the opposite direction originally and during the Ice Age its course was reversed. Its original source was a huge spring in the Sourland Mountains from which it flowed south to empty into the Delaware River near Trenton. It now flows north and empties into the Raritan River above Bound Brook. The entire valley of the Millstone is so nearly level as to make this improbable happening possible, and is now one of the few streams in the country that flow north.

Of the many little streams throughout the state the Millstone is one of the most attractive and picturesque.

A weekend camp on the shore of Lake Carnegie

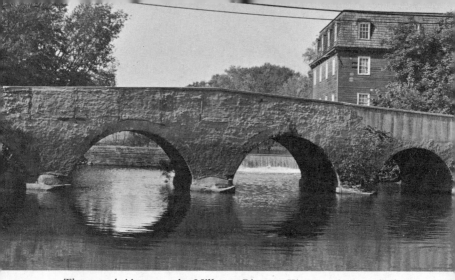

The stone bridge over the Millstone River at Kingston that was built in 1798, replacing an earlier one destroyed during the Revolutionary War. The mill, the bridge, and the surrounding area between the river and the Canal are preserved as a small state park

From Kingston to the mouth of the river near Bound Brook it is a quiet flowing stream, bordered with pleasant meadows.

The origin of the name of the river, which once may have been called "Milestone," or may have been named for a place in Scotland, is unclear, but the early settlers built a number of gristmills along its banks. The dams and many of the early tailraces are intact, but except for the mills at Kingston and Weston, none of the mill buildings still stand. The most notable characteristic of the river, particularly between Kingston and Griggstown, is the canopy of water birch trees overhead.

Because of a situation common in many of our fast-growing communities, the overloaded sewage treatment plant for the Princeton area is to some extent polluting the upper Millstone. Plans are being made, however, to enlarge the facilities and it is hoped that within a year or so the situation will be corrected.

Rockingham, Washington's Headquarters, on Route 518 at Rocky Hill

As the canoeist floats downstream he sees many reminders of the historic past of the valley. Passing under the stone arch bridge at Princeton it may be recalled that this bridge, built in 1798, replaced the one destroyed by the Continentals to delay the pursuing British after the Battle of Princeton.

Continuing downstream, the canoeist should land at the Rocky Hill Bridge and walk up the hill a mile to Rockingham, which was Washington's headquarters and residence from August 23 to November 10, 1783, while the Continental Congress was in session at Princeton. It was here that Washington wrote his farewell orders to the Army on November 2.

Rockingham, now a State Historic Site, has been faithfully restored and authentically furnished by the State, with the

The foundations of an early Griggstown grist mill on which a modern house has been built may be seen above the retaining wall on the old raceway

A Princeton YWCA canoeing group loading their canoes after an all-day cruise on the Delaware and Raritan Canal and the Millstone River. This enthusiastic group cruises a Jersey river every other Monday in the spring and summer

assistance of the Rockingham Association. It is open to the public Tuesday through Saturday, 10 A.M. to 12 noon, and 1 to 5 P.M. On Sundays the hours are 2 to 5 P.M. There is a small admission charge.

Although the Millstone traverses the north central section of New Jersey between New York and Philadelphia, the countryside visible from the river remains today little changed from fifty years ago. The commercial activities along the river have actually decreased during that time.

Following the course of the river from Princeton to Bound Brook runs the historic Delaware and Raritan Canal, to which a full chapter in this volume is devoted. At some places the river runs within a few hundred feet of the canal and at others they are only a dozen feet apart.

This scene is repeated many times throughout the winding reaches of the Millstone River from Kingston to the mouth of the stream near Manville

At Griggstown the tailrace from the river turned the wheel of a gristmill that operated for many years. Only the foundations of that mill are left and a modern house has been built on them. Here also, the house occupied by John Honeyman during the Revolution can be seen from the river. Legend has it that Honeyman was Washington's personal spy and that he supplied the information about the strength of the British in Trenton which enabled Washington to make the historic crossing of the Delaware on Christmas night in 1776.

Griggstown, like the other once busy little canal ports in the valley, still retains its charm. Many of the early houses have been restored. Along this part of the canal and continuing downriver past the old iron bridge are the meadows between the river and the canal which will one day be part of the Millstone Valley State Park from Kingston to Mill-

The Van Doren House on River Road near Millstone

Referred to on the plaque as an Indian millstone, this mortar, now in front of the Old Forge Museum, was found nearby at the site of an Indian village

34

The Old Forge on River Road, said to be the oldest continuously operated smithy in the country, began operation near the beginning of the eighteenth century and continued until 1959. It is now a museum and contains the original tools, forming blocks, and other artifacts

stone. In this area the yellow cow lilies, or candocs as they are known locally, are most noticeable. They line the banks for miles and the light green of their leaves makes a colorful contrast to the yellow flowers.

At Blackwell's Mill the mill dam is easily negotiated. The mill is long gone, but the miller's house still stands across the road. Soon the canoeist will see beyond the meadows on the left side the Van Doren house. Here Washington and his staff were quartered overnight during their retirement through the valley after the Battle of Princeton.

A short distance downstream is the village of Millstone,

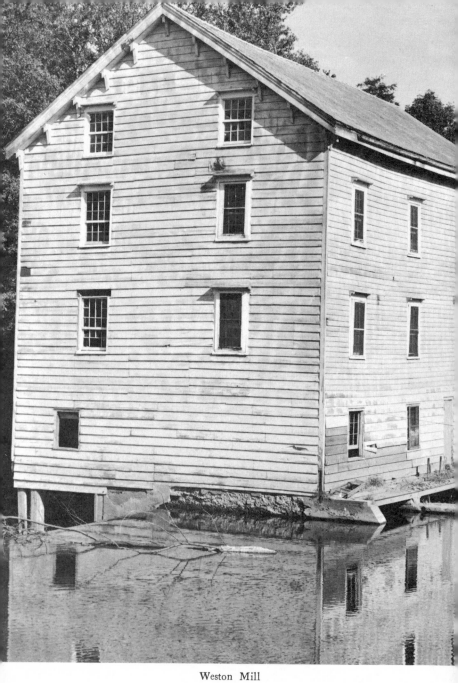

Weston Mill

originally called Somerset Court House, and one should plan to spend an hour or so here. The restored blacksmith shop contains a large collection of tools and mechanical equipment spanning two hundred years, and an anvil believed to have been brought from Holland in the 1600's. The shop is known to have been in operation from 1768 to 1959, and it is probably much older than its first authenticated date would indicate. An antique shop, gift shop, and other stores are nearby.

In the churchyard of the Dutch Reformed Church at Millstone are the graves of some of the early settlers. Nearby a marker commemorates the court house of Somerset County that was burned by Simcoe's Raiders in the Revolution. The Indian mortars, one in front of the church, the other at the forge, were found on the Van Doren farm, which is on the site of a large Indian village.

At Weston, the pre-Revolutionary gristmill still stands. The mill, known to have been in operation in 1749, was rebuilt in 1844. In 1777, a party of British foragers were defeated here in "the skirmish at Weston Mill" by several hundred militiamen under General Dickenson.

From Weston to the Raritan River, where it ends, the Millstone is too shallow for easy paddling and because of industrial activity and pollution, it is not desirable for canoeing.

Ancient rachet lift gates for controling the water flow in the chain of
lakes and the river above Mirror Lake

The Rancocas

Two small branches, together with Hanover and Mirror Lakes, above Browns Mills, both of which are within the Fort Dix Military Reservation, mark the real source of the Rancocas River. The river here is sometimes referred to as the North Branch but actually it is the main stream from its source to the Delaware River. It flows generally eastward through the two lakes to Browns Mills and from that point continues from the dam below Highway 530 and passes through New Lisbon, Pemberton, Smithville, and Mount Holly, to name the principal communities along its course. The last few miles from Mount Holly to the Delaware River is tidewater and not very suitable or interesting for canoeing.

At New Lisbon a twisting, marshy branch known as Mount Misery Creek enters the main stream on the left. This is really not much more than a large swamp brook which has its beginning in the Lebanon State Forest, with another branch north of that park near Whitesbog. The brush, growing almost down to the water, together with the swampy shores, offers few landing places for camping or picnicking. It is not pleasant canoeing water and, as a rule, is cruised only by the more adventurous who do not mind being brushwhipped, scratched by the low brush and branches, and sometimes upset.

Below Mount Holly a stream called the South Branch enters the main river. It flows from another multiple-source

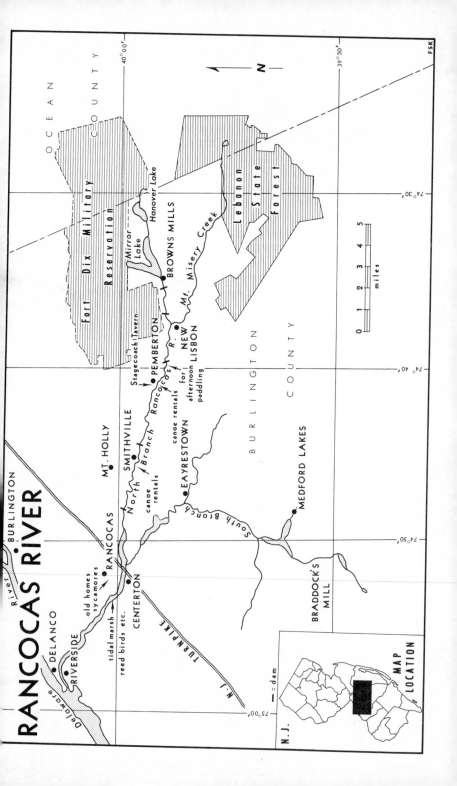

RANCOCAS RIVER

BURLINGTON

BURLINGTON COUNTY

OCEAN COUNTY

Fort Dix Military Reservation

Lebanon State Forest

Delaware River

DELANCO

RIVERSIDE

RANCOCAS

MT. HOLLY

SMITHVILLE

CENTERTON

old homes sycamores

tidal marsh

reed birds etc.

canoe rentals

North Branch

Rancocas

EAYRESTOWN

canoe rentals

South Branch

MEDFORD LAKES

BRADDOCK'S MILL

N.J. TURNPIKE

Stagecoach Tavern

PEMBERTON

Rancocas R.

canoe rentals for afternoon paddling

NEW LISBON

Mt. Misery Creek

Mirror Lake

Hanover Lake

BROWNS MILLS

N

40°00'

39°50'

74°30'

74°40'

74°50'

75°00'

0 1 2 3 4 5
miles

= dam

N.J.

MAP LOCATION

FSK

branch. Its beginnings are many, one of which starts near the Wharton State Forest, in the heart of the Pine Barrens, and another that begins near Braddock's Mill Lake. A glance at a road map will disclose how large a watershed the South Branch drains. The Rancocas is named for the Indians (variously called the Rancocas, Ankokas, or Ancocas) who lived along its shores. It was the highway of the tribes and the means of communication among their many villages. According to tradition their last great chief, Ramcoke, was buried in the Friends' Cemetery, near the bridge at Centerton. His was a funeral of state and his body was borne to its resting place in a cortege consisting of a large fleet of canoes filled with the members of his tribe.

Cruising this interesting river, on either the North or South Branches, or picnicking along its shores, it is not hard to visualize today the scene of a hundred and fifty years ago. It seems almost possible that an Indian birchbark or dugout will come around the bend in the river at any time. The spirits of the Red Men seem to hover around the countryside that was once their home. But instead of the crude canoes of the Indians one sees today the mass-production metal or plastic canoes of the white men.

The Rancocas differs in some respects from many of the South Jersey rivers but it does have much of the lovely scenery common to those streams. On its shores are many permanent homes and summer camps, but it seems wilder than it actually is, and offers mile after mile of lovely natural vistas. The heavy growth of oak and other hardwoods on both shores help create the illusion of a stream remote from civilization. The water, as is the case with other rivers that pass through the cedar swamps, is amber color.

The motorist or hiker will find it easy to explore this stream, as main highways cross it at a dozen places between

The old brick building at Pemberton that was formerly a blacksmith shop is now a storage place for Ben's Canoe rental

Browns Mills and Mount Holly. It is possible to drive along the river on Route 530, never more than a few hundred yards away from it, from Pemberton to the headwaters above Browns Mills. From Pemberton to Mount Holly a good road follows the south side of the stream. There are places to picnic, one of the most attractive being in a pine grove a hundred yards west of the bridge at New Lisbon, on the south shore.

Many people go to Pemberton, where canoes may be hired at Ben's Canoe House on the river, paddle upstream seven miles or so to the next dam at New Lisbon, and then return downstream to the starting point. It is particularly delightful in the fall when the foliage is a riot of color. If time permits, one may continue farther upstream toward the wilder area between New Lisbon and Browns Mills. Either journey can be made easily in a day.

Canoe parties, and they come to the Rancocas from as far away as Baltimore, may make arrangements at Hack's Canoe Retreat in Mount Holly to transport the craft (at their own risk) to Browns Mills or have Hack's deliver the canoes to this or other sites at an added fee, depending on the distance. It is a two-day journey from Browns Mills to Mount Holly.

Margaret Cawley cooks a meal while on a cruise down the Rancocas

The Rancocas is safe for the beginner who at least knows the rudiments of canoeing as there are few logs or other dangerous obstructions in many parts of the stream.

For the lover of bird- and wildlife the upper part of the stream is a delight. Deer, slow-moving blue heron, bittern, and ducks may be seen occasionally. It is said that the mocking bird sings in the neighborhood of Browns Mills in May. Holly and mistletoe are frequently seen.

During the middle of the last century Browns Mills was a favorite resort spot for people of New York and Philadelphia. It is lovely in the summer and it still retains its fame as a resort. A series of small lakes, created by the damming of the river, makes possible many water sports and good fishing.

The first few miles of the main stream below Browns Mills runs through such a tangle of vines and brush, and twists and turns so many times, that it actually bewilders the canoeist who travels it. Endless beauty, with surprises around every bend, is his reward.

At Pemberton there are many interesting things to see and places to visit. In the center of the village, busy by the proximity of Fort Dix, still stands the ancient stage tavern where the coaches of the eighteenth century stopped. No towns are to be seen for several miles below Pemberton, until Smithville is reached.

Some twenty-five miles or more below Browns Mills is Mount Holly, where the river explorer will want to spend some time. It is an attractive community today, but still retains much of the atmosphere of the past. Settled by Friends before 1700, it has developed into a typical modern and prosperous town and its people have apparently recognized the value of its ancient landmarks.

In the center of the town is the Burlington County Court

The Courthouse at Mt. Holly

The Mill Street Hotel in Mount Holly

House, erected in 1796, and regarded as one of the finest examples of early American architecture. The buttonwood trees in the yard were planted in 1805. The building is not open on weekends, but it and a number of other buildings in the old town are worth looking at from the outside.

Another landmark of Mount Holly is the Mill Street Hotel, part of which is the original Three Tuns Tavern of colonial days. It was built in 1723 and was an early stagecoach stop. Hessian troops were billeted there during the occupation by the British in 1776.

Few people of New Jersey know that the oldest continuously organized fire company in America is here. The first firehouse, a tiny building erected to house the leather buckets of the fire brigade in 1752, is now in the yard of one of the modern fire companies. To interested visitors the firemen will show the minute books that provide an unbroken record from the date of the founding of the first company.

Looking downstream from Mount Holly, one sees that the river is hemmed in by high banks, heavily timbered, making the stream narrower than above the town. The tide comes up as far as the Mount Holly dam and from this point to the Delaware the character of the river changes materially.

A few miles below Mount Holly the high wooded shores give way to the lowlands, bordered for the most part with rushes and other salt-water vegetation. While it is altogether different from the fresh-water reaches of the upper river, it is interesting to those who are fond of tidewater country.

Halfway between Mount Holly and the Delaware, near the right hand shore of the river, lies the town of Rancocas. The village is not old as towns go in this part of New Jersey. Few buildings date back to the beginning of the nineteenth century. However, in the surrounding countryside there are buildings erected in the early years of the eighteenth century. Among them is the John Woolman plantation, the home of the famed abolitionist, whose handsome brick manor still stands. The home of William Franklin, son of Benjamin and the last colonial governor of New Jersey, was recently torn down to make way for a new express highway. It is doubtful that the Woolman house will stand for long as the new I-95 Maine to Florida highway is being built within a hundred feet of it.

In Rancocas there are many lovely old brick houses, with the large chimney breasts on the end, so typical of eighteenth century buildings. In the center of the village is the Friends Meeting House built in 1772, before the village that now surrounds it was built.

When this Meeting House was built no village surrounded it as it does today. It is now the center of the charming village of Rancocas and weekly services and church school are still held here

The people of this lovely little community are proud of it and recently, when the New Jersey Highway Department wanted to widen the principal street through the village the outraged residents obtained over two thousand signatures to a petition of protest and made the state officials change their minds about the necessity for the project. A by-pass now under construction will serve the motorist just as well.

Under today's conditions of the over-use of the environment by too many people, particularly along the lower part of the Rancocas, including the cottagers in residence, heavy weekend traffic on the many roads that cross the stream, picnickers and the like, we suggest that in the summer pleasanter canoeing waters are from the source of the river at Hanover Lake and through the following chain of lakes and river to Browns Mills. Then continue on the river to New Lisbon. Such a cruise will give anyone plenty of paddling and comparatively quiet cruising waters.

Below Browns Mills the river is fast, and at times somewhat blocked with brush and timber, but few houses are visible from the water.

Above Browns Mills the chain of lakes and the river connecting them are for the most part within the Fort Dix Military Reservation. Surprisingly little junk or litter spoils this area. Perhaps this is partly due to the Military Reservation regulations, but the cleanliness, without the usual envi-

This swamp, in the heart of the Fort Dix Military Reservation, is the source of the main Rancocas River, sometimes referred to as the West Branch. From here to Browns Mills, Hanover, and Mirror Lake together with the river form the delightful and interesting chain of waterways

It is a delight on any summer day to paddle along the heavily forested shores of Hanover Lake as seen here above one of the water control gates

ronmental spoilage, is also due in large part to the evident pride and civic-mindedness of the people who live in the area.

Recently, as we drove around an attractive, pine-covered housing area on the north shore of Mirror Lake, above Browns Mills, we came upon a Chamber of Commerce roadside sign that read:

> Let no man say, and say it to your shame,
> That all was beauty here until you came.

The Mullica

Copper-hued faces, topped by feathered headdresses, are no longer seen among the trees on the shores of the Mullica, and yet it would seem perfectly natural to find Indians still roaming through the area. Near here, on one of the earliest Indian Reservations, established in 1758, the last of the New Jersey Indians lived. They were well housed and had plenty of acreage in which to hunt and fish but they were not happy. In 1801 they sold their land and moved to the Oneida Indian Reservation in northern New York State. One member of the tribe, known as Indian Ann, remained on the Reservation in New Jersey and lived to be more than a hundred years old.

Atsion, originally called Atsayunk, was named for a local tribe of Indians. Another group adopted the name of Mullica and so honored their friend and patron, Eric Mullica, who settled his Swedish colony on the shores of the river in 1697.

The Mullica was one of the shore rivers to which Indians from as far away as Minisink Island on the upper Delaware River made annual visits to feast on the oysters for which the river was famed. Today, in places along the shores and on some of the islands, heaps of shells remain as evidences of those early visits.

As one paddles quietly down the upper reaches of the river the journey is through really wild forest lands. From Highway 206, all the way to Sweetwater, the stream is within the Wharton State Forest. There are no buildings or

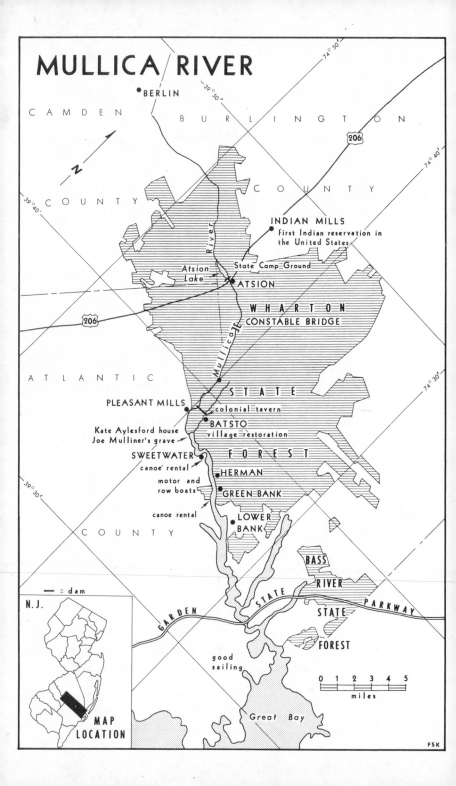

MULLICA RIVER

BERLIN

CAMDEN

BURLINGTON

206

N

COUNTY

COUNTY

River

INDIAN MILLS
first Indian reservation in
the United States

Atsion
Lake

State Camp Ground

ATSION

206

WHARTON

CONSTABLE BRIDGE

ATLANTIC

Mullica

STATE

PLEASANT MILLS

colonial tavern

BATSTO

village restoration

Kate Aylesford house
Joe Mulliner's grave

SWEETWATER

FOREST

canoe rental

HERMAN

motor and
row boats

GREEN BANK

canoe rental

LOWER
BANK

COUNTY

BASS

RIVER

STATE

PARKWAY

STATE

FOREST

— = dam

N.J.

GARDEN

STATE

good
sailing

MAP
LOCATION

0 1 2 3 4 5
miles

Great Bay

FSK

Casting for pickerel while on a canoe trip down river from Constable
Bridge

At times a saw or small axe makes the going a bit easier on the rivers of the Pine Barrens. (Arthur Mueller photo)

settlements along the way. The spiritual presence of the first Americans seems somehow to pervade the whole area.

Unlike most other Pine Barrens waterways, the Mullica cannot be easily explored by car as only sand roads parallel both sides of it from its source down to tidewater. The only part of the river that can be safely explored by car is that area along the north shore of Atsion Lake (a couple of miles of the stream that have been made into a lake) and the area below Sweetwater where modern roads permit following the river to the ocean.

For those who have the experience and stamina, a good starting place is just below Atsion Lake and Route 206. At that point the river is narrow and fast and sometimes blocked with brush and fallen trees. A bit of work with an axe or saw may be necessary to get through to the more open water below. Once having begun a trip, however, there is no return except on foot along a sand road, if you can find one. The Atsion Lake starting point calls for seven or eight hours of paddling to reach Sweetwater.

For the less experienced, or anyone preferring an easier cruise, plan to start at Constable Bridge. From there to Keller's Marina is only a few hours' paddle, allowing plenty of time for some pickerel fishing and lunch on the way down.

If you have a jeep or other four-wheel-drive car it is possible to drive to Constable Bridge. Otherwise it may prove less expensive to have someone like Elmer Keller drive you and your canoe there in his truck. Your car can be left at

Somewhere on the way to Constable Bridge. It was necessary to negotiate a treacherous sand road in a truck to get the party to their starting point

his marina and picked up at the end of the cruise. If you rent a canoe from Mr. Keller he will take your group and the required number of canoes to whatever starting point you choose. He knows the conditions on the river and can be helpful to those unfamiliar with the region.

Perhaps some day the local sand roads will be surfaced, but we hope not, as that would spoil the clean wilderness it is possible to enjoy now.

For those of you who have never negotiated one of the Pine Barren sand roads and worse yet had your axle buried in the powdery sand, we urge you not to try it. We make it a practice, before trying to take our two-wheel-drive car over any unfamiliar sand road, to look up the park ranger at Batsto Village and ask him if it is possible. If he advises against trying it, take his advice.

In addition to the Mullica River Marina there are several good canoe rentals along the lower Mullica. The proprietors know the river and conditions and with their six- or eight-canoe trailers can supply as many canoes as may be needed.

During the spring when there is plenty of water it is possible to float down the river. One has to keep alert, however, as the fast current, sweeping around the bends, sometimes under overhanging brush or down timber, can be disastrous or can at least split a paddle. On this trip an extra paddle or two may be good insurance. A small camp saw or axe may prove helpful in some places.

As would be expected, this wild paradise is full of many kinds of game. Deer, grouse, and quail are plentiful. According to hunters and local game officials the wild turkey that was once so abundant is now staging a comeback. So now we have once again both the cranberries and the wild turkey as they were before the advent of the white man.

On a recent cruise in early May, the profusion of wild

This view of an unspoiled natural environment of marsh and forest at
Constable Bridge on the Mullica is typical of the region

plants and flowers was a delight. That rare water plant, the
golden spike, was well above the surface of the river and
the intriguing fiddlehead ferns could be seen everywhere
along the river. The pure white seashore sand, sometimes
to a height of from three to ten feet above the river, was in
vivid contrast to the green of the pine and cedar forest above,
reminding us that all of New Jersey was under the ocean
at one time.

As we paddled along during that early spring cruise we
agreed that sometime, perhaps in October, we would again
cruise the Mullica but make it a two- or three-day trip,
camping overnight on some of those delightful sandy shores.

The Mullica River played a dramatic part in the Revolutionary War. Pleasant Mills was at that time an important
industrial center. In fact, during the blockade of New York

Starting a cruise down the Mullica from Constable Bridge

and Philadelphia by the British, the nearby Batsto forges and furnaces were the chief source of cannonballs for the Continental Army.

When the British realized their blockade was not a success they decided to send gunboats up the Mullica, destroy the fleet of American privateers on the way, and then burn the Batsto works. In the ensuing engagement between the British and American fleets, the British were attacked not only by the American sea forces but were hammered by the cannons of the militia from the shore. It was evident the British plans would not succeed.

Having been whipped at what has since been known as the battle of Chestnut Neck, the British did not again attempt to take the Batsto works. Batsto continued to supply the Continental forces with ammunition throughout the Revolutionary War.

Bride and groom trees flanking the entrance to the Manor off Highway
542 in Pleasant Mills. Tradition has it that they were planted for Honoria
Reid, the daughter of the Batsto Village Ironmaster, in 1754

59

Marker over the grave of the reputed "Robin Hood" of the Pine Barrens
in the woods beside Highway 542 near Sweetwater

The community of Pleasant Mills was a favorite haunt
of the Indians. There is a lake of some size which the Indians
knew as Nescochague. On its shores stands the imposing
manor house, built in 1754.

There is a great deal of interest and romance around the
manor that dates back to the eighteenth century. The owner's
daughter, Honoria Reid, is said to have been the heroine of
Peterson's novel dealing with the historic background of the
section which was published under the title of *Kate Aylesford*.
The novel enjoyed wide popularity many years ago. It told of
the adventures of Kate, who was seized by the notorious Pine
Barrens robber, Joe Mulliner, and held for ransom. She was
eventually rescued by local citizens led by a British officer—
whom she later married, of course. The exploits of Mulliner

Clark's Landing, seven miles below Pleasant Mills on the Mullica River, was settled near the beginning of the eighteenth century and became a community of over fifty homes within a few years. No trace of the settlement remains and the site is now a state picnic and boat launching park

and his gang of "refugees," as they styled themselves, are still being talked about in this region. We were regaled with several of these yarns by the proprietor of the Sweetwater Casino on the river, while lunching there during a recent canoe cruise. It is said that some of the local people regarded this outlaw as a modern Robin Hood. To the majority, however, he was just a bandit.

Joe and his gang operated along the shores of the Mullica for many years, during which his depredations ranged from petty thievery to large-scale robbery. We were told how his many successes led to greater boldness and, despite the price on his head, he began to appear at dances and other social functions. On one such occasion a special reception was planned for him by a group of outraged citizenry, with the result that on a summer evening in 1781 the bold bandit was captured and hanged to a nearby tree. They buried him near the road and a monument now marks the spot.

The broad reaches of the lower Mullica and the plentiful supply of pine and oak were a natural combination for the development of the shipbuilding industry one hundred and fifty years ago. Shipyards lined both shores all the way to Great Bay, and in them were built some of the famous Clipper ships.

The last twelve miles of this river is decidedly not water for cruising in a canoe unless one is accustomed to the vagaries of wind-swept salt-water. It is delightful sailing or powerboat water, and special boat trips are arranged for parties who want to see the river or stop in at one of the casinos along the way.

The Wading

The Wading River, long known to experienced canoeists as one of the wildest and most beautiful of the Pine Barren streams, has its beginnings in several small branches, both to the east and to the west of Chatsworth. On those branches are several small cranberry bogs. Because of the swamps and sometimes heavy stands of cedar, that part of the river above Speedwell on Route 563 is usually choked with fallen timber and brush and cruising it is not practical. It calls for a lot of hard work with axe and saw.

Many canoe clubs, including the Mohawk, Murray Hill, Sierra, Rutgers Outing, Appalachian, and Green Mountain clubs schedule cruises on the Wading every spring and fall. They keep the river below Speedwell pretty well cleared of obstacles, including the more recent beaver dams. Whenever one of the beaver dams or other obstruction is encountered it is easily cleared away or carried around. We don't mind the little effort to negotiate them as they seem to be a part of the wild nature of the river.

It is possible to get lost on this river by inadvertently paddling up a dead-end channel that may lead to nowhere. We suggest to those who may like an easy day's cruise, that they launch their canoe from Highway 563, four miles south of the general store in the center of Chatsworth. From that point to the best place to take the canoes out of the river again is about sixteen miles by water but only about six by road. Driving south on 563, past Jenkins and taking the

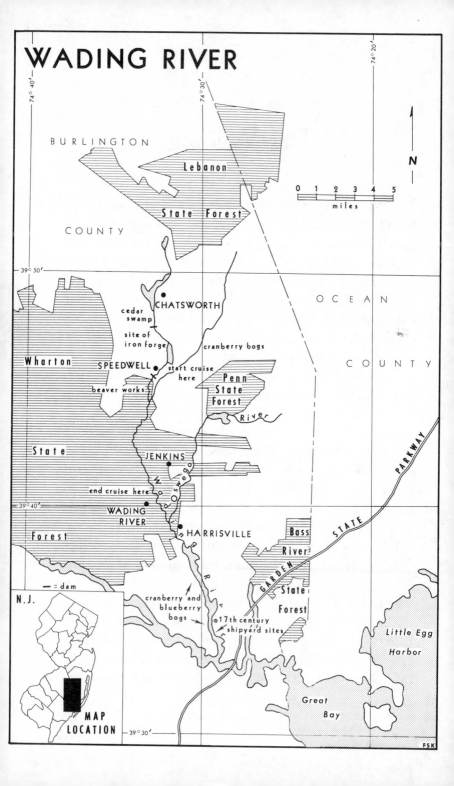

WADING RIVER

BURLINGTON

Lebanon

State   Forest

COUNTY

OCEAN

CHATSWORTH

cedar
swamp

site of
iron forge

cranberry bogs

COUNTY

Wharton

SPEEDWELL

start cruise
here

Penn
State
Forest

beaver works

River

State

JENKINS

end cruise here

WADING
RIVER

HARRISVILLE

Bass

River

State

Forest

cranberry and
blueberry
bogs

17th century
shipyard sites

Little Egg
Harbor

== = dam

N.J.

GARDEN   STATE   PARKWAY

Great
Bay

MAP
LOCATION

0 1 2 3 4 5
miles

N

FSK

Unlike the Oswego River with its fast-flowing water from the lake to Harrisville, much of the Wading above the cranberry bogs is often blocked as shown here, and some work is required to remove the debris in order to get through

Cutting a passage through the down timber above Speedwell on that first cruise on the Wading, when the cruisers lost their river

right fork in the road, a short distance below the fork the road again crosses the river. There is a nice shelving beach above the bridge to take the canoes out and plenty of safe parking space off the road. To continue beyond this point is to battle with more open water, wind, and tide.

Those who may want transportation and/or to rent canoes for a cruise on this or other nearby streams will find The Belle Haven Lake Camp and Rental the nearest facility not only for canoes but for cabins or other overnight accommodations. Mr. Belle can suggest the best places to start and end a canoe trip and he knows the area and conditions well.

In order to enjoy the wild beauty of this stream it is necessary to journey down it by canoe. The traveler by car, however, may reach it at many points along the roads that run near the river, or cross it frequently.

On a brilliant fall Saturday many years ago we decided to try a cruise from the very headwaters, at the lake near Chatsworth. We had no reason to believe such a trip could be made except for general information that there appeared to be enough water to float a canoe. We reckoned without the tangle of fallen cedar trees through which we had much additional exercise in the form of axe work for the first five miles. From the start of the cruise we were surrounded with a profusion of white cedar, laurel, and other species of plants and great trees. Thousands of acres of beautiful aromatic cedars lined the shores with an impenetrable swampland extending for miles on both sides. It was a scene of indescribable beauty, and during the entire morning journey we did not see a single sign of civilization along the way.

Between eight o'clock and one we had progressed a distance of not more than five miles because of the difficulties of getting through the down timber. It seemed as if we were off in some faraway wilderness instead of within a few miles

The majestic Atlantic white cedars that are a prominent feature of the Wading River have been described as "appearing like rows of toy wooden soldiers, marching along the river"

of busy state highways. And that was not the last of our adventures that day. Before we finished our trip we enjoyed the experience of actually becoming lost, with only an hour of daylight left to find our way out to the highway. More about that later on in the story.

One of the best descriptions written about these cedar swamps may be found in *American Ornithology* by Alexander Wilson, written more than a hundred years ago. He wrote:

The appearance they [the white cedar trees] present to a stranger is singular—a front of tall and perfectly straight trunks, rising to a height of fifty or sixty feet, without a limb, and crowded in every direction, their tops so closely woven together as to shut out the day, spreading the gloom of a perpetual twilight below. On a nearer approach, they are found to rise out of the water, which from the impregnation of the fallen leaves and roots of the cedars, is the color of brandy. Amidst this bottom of congregated springs, the ruins of the former forest life lie piled in every state of confusion. The roots, prostrate logs, and in many places, the water, are covered with green, mantling moss, while an undergrowth of laurel, fifteen or twenty feet high, intersects every opening so completely as to render passage through laborious and harassing beyond description; at every step, you either sink to the knees, clamber over fallen timber, squeeze yourself through between the stubborn laurels, or plunge to the middle in ponds made by the uprooting of large trees, which the green moss concealed from observation. In calm weather the silence of death reigns in these dreary regions; a few interrupted rays of light shoot across the gloom; and but for the occasional hollow screams of the herons, and the melancholy chirping of one or two species of small birds, all is silence, solitude, and desolation. When a breeze rises, at first it sighs mournfully through the tops; but as the gale increases, the tall mast-like cedars wave like fishing poles, and rubbing against each other produce a variety of singular noises that, with the help of a little imagination, resemble shrieks, groans, growling bears, wolves, and such like comfortable sounds.

The general description of the eerie qualities of the cedars and laurels still holds, but of course the giant cedars Wilson mentions have been cut over during the past hundred years.

On the cruise we started out to describe we finally managed to get to a main road by one o'clock and, since we could not find any dry land elsewhere, we sat on the edge of the road to eat our lunch.

Questioning a passing native we learned that the river was more open below us and that we would not have much trouble—except getting through a large cranberry bog a few miles below. By the time we arrived at the bog, after resuming our trip, we began to worry a bit about reaching our destina-

An unusual view of the Wading River below Speedwell where the stream
runs wide and clear of debris

tion before dark. Arrangements had been made to have a
man drive our car to a point we had hoped to reach at the
end of the day.

Our stream spread out into a wide bayou and below was the
mile-long dike. Beaching the canoe, we went up to look it
over, and since it was crossed with a system of irrigation
ditches, we could not decide which of them would take us
through the bog to the river again. We finally decided on a
channel to the left of the bog and started to work our way
through it. The sun was getting lower and it appeared that
we might have to spend a cold night on the river. Such an
experience would not have been a new one but it certainly
would not have been comfortable in late October without
blankets.

Paddling through a narrow, brush-covered opening, we found the going fairly good, only to discover, from the way the grass on the river bottom pointed, that we were paddling upstream. Retracing our route we came into what appeared to be a larger stream and soon had to carry around a bog floodgate. Below the gate the river ran clear and fast and our difficulties seemed to be over.

Rounding a bend we swung into a large pondlike area. To our utter confusion the water then proceeded to circle the

Typical of the charcoal burning operations in the Pine Barrens until the last cone was fired in 1963

Timber charcoal burned near Speedwell in the Pine Barrens. It was made of the yellow pine of the Wading River area and for cook-outs is far superior to the briquets that are made of coal dust and oil

pond and there did not seem to be any outlet. The entire shoreline failed to show any sign of the river continuing and so we had to go back to the gate. Fifteen minutes or so of daylight remained and we decided to leave the canoe and try to get out to a road while the light lasted. Following a narrow path we reached a sand road and finally a main highway. A walk of two miles brought us to the river again and our car driver who was patiently waiting.

We never did find out why we lost the river that day—whether it went underground or whether we had wandered into one of the many blind channels so common in the swamplands. The perplexing question remains as to why the river flowed so strongly to that dead end pond and point of its disappearance.

Since that first attempt to cruise the river we have run it many times but have never again got out of the main stream of the river and into the false channels as we apparently did the first time. No one has any difficulty today in keeping to the proper channel from Speedwell downstream.

Until a few years ago, in this part of the Pine Barrens, a very interesting, centuries-old industry flourished. The art of charcoal burning had been handed down from father to son for many generations in some cases. The operator first leased pine acreage and began cutting the timber with which the truncated cones were constructed. This then was covered with clay and the pile was ignited. Depending upon the strength and direction of the wind, holes were poked at various places and, if the operator had practiced the art correctly, a pile of charcoal resulted after a week of burning. The operation required such careful control that it had to be watched day and night or just a pile of useless ashes would be the result of the week's work.

According to the state forester, no charcoal burning has been done in the Barrens since 1963.

There is a fascination in the exploration of this pitch-pine and cedar country that is different from any other part of the state. There is so much actual wilderness and so many interesting things to see that it is hard to believe the area is a part of the densely populated state of New Jersey. Good roads are plentiful everywhere and it is not necessary to risk getting stuck in one of the treacherous sand roads that may be found throughout the Barrens.

The pungent odor of the pines and cedars in the hot sun will stay in your memory for days after a visit.

Below the cedar swamps on the Wading River the country changes in character as the salt tidewater is reached. Wide areas of salt marsh are the rule, and during the fall literally thousands of ducks and geese are seen. Great areas of the Wading River are devoted to the cultivation of blueberries and cranberries; the crops are the mainstay of the locality.

For the uninitiated canoeist we would suggest that trips be planned for the early fall months on this river, as in summer insects are abundant in the swampland. In any event the fall color makes it far more beautiful and the crisp air makes paddling more enjoyable.

The Maurice

The Maurice River offers a wide variety of beauty and many places of interest to the explorers of the little streams of New Jersey. Like most South Jersey rivers its actual beginning is hard to find. There are four branches—two start near Glassboro, another north of Clayton, and a fourth near Cross Keys. The last is known as Scotland Run. The two western branches come together a short distance below Franklinville and form the Maurice proper. Despite the spelling of the name local folks pronounce it as if it were spelled Morris. A few miles below Franklinville, at Malaga, Scotland Run adds its flow to the main stream.

The motorist will find this river fairly easy to explore as it is a simple matter to get to any part of it. The canoeist, however, should confine his cruising to the part between Malaga or Willow Grove and Millville. It is of course possible to paddle a canoe all the way to Delaware Bay but the tide and other conditions make it unattractive below Millville.

One of the unusual features of this river is Union Lake, which was created by a dam at Millville. The water of the stream is backed up into a lake nearly four miles long, said to be the largest wholly artificial lake in New Jersey. Despite the fact that it is artificial, the uneven shores, with high cliffs of clay on the west shore and the little islands, combine to make this an attractive lake.

At the head of the stream in Glassboro one may still find

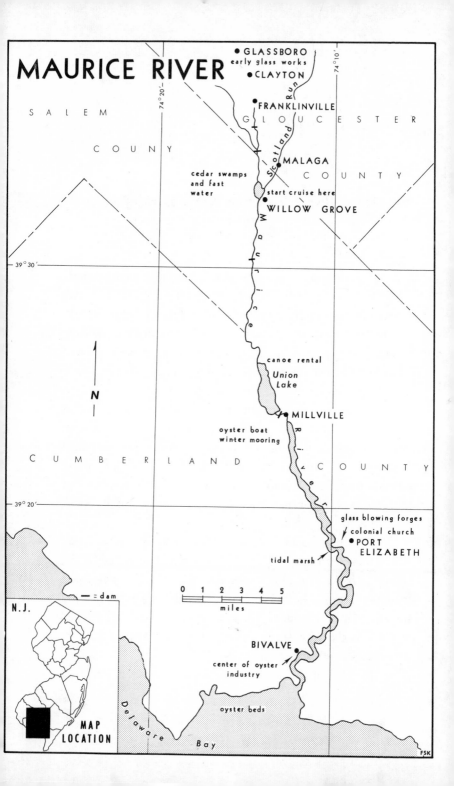

A few of the fleet of oyster boats moored at Port Norris on the lower Maurice. The present-day fleet numbers only about fifty boats that regularly begin harvesting oysters in Delaware Bay in the fall. At one time, when all the boats depended upon sail, hundreds of them were in service

77

Near the headwaters of one of the several branches of this river it is difficult to find a clear passage for the canoe, except during the higher waters of spring

the evidence of the onetime prosperous industry of glass blowing. This industry had its start in America over two hundred years ago at Allaway and shortly after the Revolution was moved to Glassboro, where it was carried on until very recently. The famous Wistar and Stanger glass had its early beginnings nearby, and the surrounding countryside is filled with the descendants of the early Germans who founded this great industry in America.

On some parts of the upper reaches of the three branches of the Maurice are still found a few small dams, some of which were built a century or more ago, to flood bogs and to supply power for the early gristmills. Above each of the dams is a little lake, some of which are remarkably beautiful sheets of water. For example, above the dam at Fries Mill on Scotland Run is an area of perfectly blue water, an unusual sight in this part of New Jersey where most of the water is amber-colored. This sheet of water is backed with acres of cedars and pines which provide a rich contrast and enhance the natural beauty of the blue water and of the skies reflected in it. It is such unexpected bits of loveliness that make the exploration of our rivers so delightful an experience.

From Malaga, where many cruisers start their journeys, to the lake east of Willow Grove the Maurice runs fast, at times at the rate of six miles or more an hour. The speed of the foam-flecked amber water, rushing the canoeist around the bends and calling for fast work with the paddle at times, provides a real thrill. As the stream merges into the lake the journey is slowed down a bit, but soon after the dam at the

A part of the attractive east shore of the pond on Scotland Run, one of the many tributaries of the Maurice

foot of the lake is portaged the speed of the water becomes evident again. Many parties start their journey at this point, obtaining canoes at Millville or carrying their own on top of their cars. By road the distance to Millville is not over ten miles, but it is more than twice that by water. However, the fast-running water enables one to make the voyage to the head of Union Lake in an afternoon if necessary. It is better to plan to devote a whole day, permitting stops for the enjoyment of the woods and colorful foliage. In places the cedars and pines form a solid green arch overhead, sometimes coming down so close to the water as to make it difficult to get through. On the upper river, particularly, it seems like emerging from a tunnel to pass from the heavy forested areas to the sunlit parts of the stream, with the bright sun of early summer dancing on the water. Everywhere the odor of white cedar fills the air.

Southwest of Vineland the river widens out and soon changes character. The close intimacy of the little stream and the crowding forest give way to the sandy shores of Union Lake. The flood of cedar water is lost in the larger area of the blue water of the lake. A few small islands help give the impression of a natural lake, as do the sand beaches along its shores. On the east shore are many summer cottages and the usual recreational facilities, but they do not detract from the natural charm of the lake itself. Motorists may drive across the head and the foot of the lake but it is necessary to seek out the wood roads to get to the more isolated parts of the shore.

At the lower end of the lake the cruiser must decide whether he should terminate his trip or face a long carry around the dam and mills and then buck the tide of the lower river. There is plenty of interest below this point, but the comparatively uninteresting miles of salt marsh that line

Early morning reflections along the shore of the lower Maurice

the shores make it advisable to finish the exploration along the river to Delaware Bay by car.

Below Millville the river again changes character. It is difficult to believe that the stream is the same one that begins at Glassboro. There are many scenes reminiscent of Gloucester, Massachusetts, along the part of the river that extends from Millville to the bay. Hundreds of masts are silhouetted against the sky line, but, instead of fishing boats, there are the famous oyster shallops. In the early fall the oyster fleet is the scene of great activity in the fitting out and overhauling for the oyster season. Many of the ship-

Chief Hydrographic Engineer L. Albertson Huber demonstrating the use
of the oyster tongs

yards, which are now devoted largely to the building and repair of the oyster boats, have been in operation since colonial days.

On the way to Bivalve are such places as Mauricetown, Port Norris, Buckshutem, Port Elizabeth, and others with names of English origin. Here and there stands a red-brick house of the colonial period. From Port Elizabeth famous clipper ships sailed out over the seven seas, less than a hundred and fifty years ago. The development of railroads and modern highways has done much to spoil the charm of this community, but many of the early buildings remain. The old church, built in 1827, is surrounded by a cemetery that dates back to 1786. In the neighborhood of Mauricetown one may see miles of the dikes built by early settlers to reclaim the rich bottomland.

At Bivalve, where the Maurice ends its journey to the sea, there is a great deal to interest the visitor. The name of the town is obviously derived from its chief industry. Out in Delaware Bay lie the great oyster beds, the result of years of careful planting and conservation.

These oyster beds were recognized as an important natural resource as early as 1719. To prevent their spoilage regulatory laws were passed early in the nineteenth century.

As recently as 1950 the oyster harvesting and processing industry in Bivalve and vicinity carried a capital investment that ran into millions of dollars. Oysters were brought in with a value of almost $3 million, and the 150 boats were valued at around $25,000 each. Add to this the value of fourteen shucking houses, waterfront property, docks, etc. In the early years of the century most of the oyster boats were under sail, and until 1945 dredging in the seed beds was permitted only by sailboats. This was a conservation measure as sailboats are relatively inefficient dredgers.

The oyster museum established by Mr. Huber in his office at Bivalve is the focal point of most visitors to the oyster fisheries headquarters at the mouth of the Maurice River

The oyster producing areas of Delaware Bay are divided into three parts: the lower 35,000 acres are leased grounds on which individuals raise and harvest market oysters; the upper bay area contains the state-controlled natural seed beds from which the oyster planters obtain seed oysters in the spring to place on this leased ground; and the tongers areas are shoal waters reserved for the use of small operators, who harvest with long-handled tongs from the sterns or sides of their boats.

Around 1957, a deadly disease called MSX attacked the oyster beds and reduced the harvest to practically nothing. Methods of control have been developed and the beds are again being seeded. Mr. L. Albertson Huber, chief hydrographic engineer in the state Division of Fish, Game, and

Shell Fisheries, who supervises the seeding and harvesting operation, told us that the industry is making a good comeback and future crops should approach their former magnitude.

During our tour with Mr. Huber we were shown the great shucking and packing sheds in which the oysters are received, counted, and shucked for shipment. The shells are conveyed to the large piles outside to be sold later.

To us the most fascinating feature of our visit was Mr. Huber's special pride, his oyster museum. Here are displayed many specimens of marine life, bottles and branches of trees to which the oyster attaches itself, and many other marine oddities. It is decidedly worth a visit during the harvesting season and it might be possible to wangle "a dozen on the half-shell."

While the last few miles of the Maurice are not at all suited to canoe cruising, the reader will find it extremely interesting to make arrangements with one of the power-boatmen at Millville to journey down to Bivalve and along-shore to see this industry in operation. It is also possible to drive right to the packing and shipping sheds and walk through, observing the fascinating array of oystering gear and the handling of the crop from the boats through to its actual packing. The men who operate the shore end of the business are obliging in permitting visitors to watch their operations.

The later afternoon, when the boats are moored for the night, offers unusual opportunities for marine photographs and scenes that will make the artist reach for his brushes.

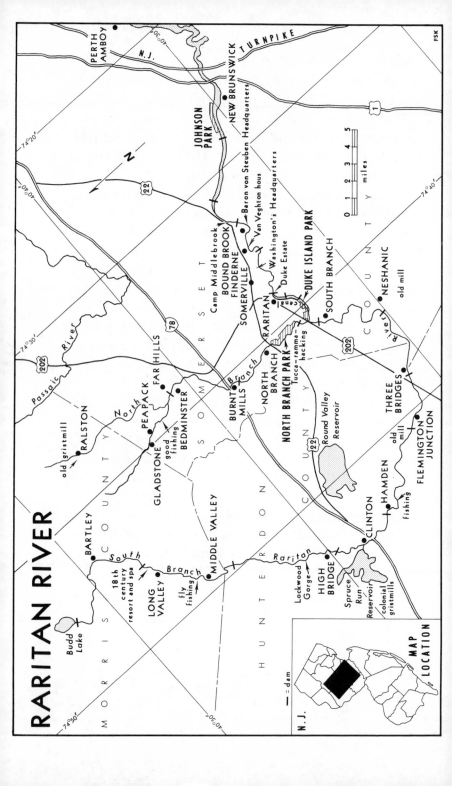

RARITAN RIVER

FSK

N.J.

PERTH AMBOY

TURNPIKE

NEW BRUNSWICK

JOHNSON PARK

N

22

Baron von Steuben Headquarters

Van Veghton hous

Washington's Headquarters

Camp Middlebrook

BOUND BROOK

FINDERNE

Duke Estate

SOMERVILLE

DUKE ISLAND PARK

RARITAN

Canal

SOUTH BRANCH

NESHANIC

old mill

SOMERSET COUNTY

78

Branch

202

North

FAR HILLS

BURNT MILLS

NORTH BRANCH

NORTH BRANCH PARK

Tucca-ramma-hacking

River

THREE BRIDGES

202

PEAPACK

good fishing

BEDMINSTER

Round Valley Reservoir

Passaic River

RALSTON

old gristmill

GLADSTONE

MIDDLE VALLEY

22

FLEMINGTON JUNCTION

HAMDEN

old mill

fishing

CLINTON

BARTLEY

South

Branch

LONG VALLEY

fly fishing

Raritan

Lockwood Gorge

HIGH BRIDGE

HUNTERDON COUNTY

Spruce Run Reservoir

colonial gristmills

MORRIS COUNTY

18th century resort and spa

Budd Lake

= dam

N.J.

MAP LOCATION

0 1 2 3 4 5 miles

The Raritan—South Branch
and North Branch

Why the early geographers chose to designate that part of the river from its source at Budd Lake to its meeting with the North Branch as the South Branch, and from that point on to Raritan Bay as the Raritan is a mystery. Those who have explored the valleys of these streams by car or by canoe will agree that from the nature of the terrain, size, and water flow, they appear to be one river. Counting this as one stream, we have the longest river in New Jersey, over one hundred miles from its source to Raritan Bay.

The Raritan has always appealed to poets and other writers, and probably more has been written about its beauty and commercial possibilities than has appeared in print about any other waterway in the state. In 1806, John Davis, an English poet, described this lovely river in his "Ode to the Raritan, Queen of Rivers":

> All thy wat'ry face
>   Reflected with a purer grace,
> Thy many turnings through the trees,
>   Thy bitter journey to the seas,
> Thou Queen of Rivers, Raritan!

As far back as 1683 Thomas Rudyard, in his book on the American Colonies, mentioned the Raritan as a river that would probably assume large importance in the commerce of the Colonies. Peter Kalm, a visiting Swedish scholar, in his book of impressions of this country, said that this river would one day be the chief water highway in America, and he also wrote at length of the beauty of the upper part of the river.

The name Raritan came from the Indian word Laletan, meaning "forked river." Another interpretation is "smooth running" or "gentle." The Indian villages of the Naraticongs were scattered all along the shores of the river and on it they plied their canoes from its headwaters to the bay. They used the Raritan as their chief artery of travel by canoe until the middle of the eighteenth century and their trails followed both shores. The final act of purchase of the Indian rights and lands, before the last of the New Jersey tribes were moved to reservations, was concluded on the banks of this river.

In 1650 Cornelius van Tienhoven, Secretary of the West India Company, wrote:

The district inhabited by a nation called the Raritangs is situated on a fresh water river that flows through the center of a lowland which the Indians cultivated. This is the handsomest and pleasantest country that man can behold. It furnished the Indians with an abundance of maize, beans, pumpkins and other fruits. . . . Through the valley pass large numbers of all sorts of tribes, on their way north or east. The land is, therefore, not only adapted for raising grain and rearing cattle, but also is very convenient for trade with the Indians.

The settlers who came to the valley, after van Tienhoven's report was made public in Holland, soon settled throughout the length of the Raritan. They harnessed the waters of the river to drive the wheels of countless gristmills, and although few traces of those industries remain, the original charm and peacefulness of the river are still evident.

Those thrifty and hardworking Dutch built substantial fortunes from the farms and mills and today many of their

Low dams like this one are occasionally encountered and offer no difficulties, as the canoe can be lined over them, and in the spring the water is usually high enough to run them

The shallow, fast water through the ravine opposite Duke's Island Park is a very attractive section of the Raritan

descendants are still carrying on the agricultural pursuits of their forebears, particularly in Hunterdon County. Unlike most other New Jersey counties, Hunterdon is still predominately rural in character. Fifty percent of Hunterdon County acreage is still cultivated on fourteen hundred farms.

THE SOUTH BRANCH

The South Branch, particularly, still retains that aristocratic poise that gives it a character different from that of any other river in the east. Before the surrounding lands were denuded of their heavy forests the river was deeper than it is now. As late as 1750 large flatboats were poled upstream as far as Raritan and then floated back to the storehouses at New Brunswick, with the flour and other mill products of the upper river.

Starting in the hills of Morris County as an outlet from Budd Lake, the South Branch winds its leisurely way in and out of the valley, twisting and turning to avoid the hills for the first few miles, and then straightening out its course as it flows southeast past Schooleys Mountain. It runs through the quiet little villages of Bartley, Naughright, Long and Middle Valley, and then quickens its pace as it weaves its way through the hills to High Bridge. To this point the river is too shallow to attempt any canoe cruising, although we have negotiated it on the high water in the spring. In fact, it affords an exciting run in time of high water, but it should not be attempted by a beginner. The five miles through the deep ravine from Hoffman's to Lockwood Gorge, above High Bridge, become dangerous when the water is high enough to run there, because of the huge boulders that practically fill the river. It is better to explore the first twenty miles by car or by walking along the more isolated spots.

The South Branch is a favorite stream of the trout fisherman. It is kept well stocked with adult-size trout and good sport is the result. There is a great deal to interest the lover of scenic beauty, as well as the fisherman.

At High Bridge the river breaks through the last of the mountains, and formerly a beautiful waterfall could be seen where the seventy-five-foot power dam now stands. On the eastern shore, below the dam, is the Taylor Wharton Iron and Steel Company, the oldest continuously operated iron works in the state. Deposits of iron in the hills surrounding the town, and a plentiful supply of timber for charcoal, as well as water power, made a natural combination for the start of this industry in 1742.

After breaking through the mountains at High Bridge, the river, as if to catch its breath from the tumultuous run through the rock-strewn gap, slows down to a wandering

One of the two eighteenth-century grist mills in Clinton. This one, with its operating water wheel, now houses the Clinton Museum, which has an interesting collection of Americana

meadow stream. In all but seasons of very dry weather those who wish to paddle a canoe on the South Branch can safely launch their boat anywhere between High Bridge and Clinton. There are some dams and shallows, however.

The South Branch from below High Bridge to Flemington Junction and beyond has become very popular with canoeing groups in recent years. It affords a delightful day of sun and recreation through the hills of Hunterdon County. Some canoeists cruise all the way to Landing Bridge, above New Brunswick, taking three or more days and camping along the river on the journey.

The South Branch Watershed Association sponsors and conducts cruises from Clinton to Darts Mills at Flemington Junction every weekend during the canoeing season.

Until the Spruce Run Reservoir, west of the river above Clinton, was built and the pumping of water from the river began we had no difficulty with low water except during prolonged dry spells. Since the pumping began, however, seeming at times almost to pump the stream dry, our canoe journeys have been more wading than paddling. Thanks to the persistent efforts of the South Branch Watershed Association the State has agreed to stop the pumping on Saturdays and Sundays. It is therefore advisable, in planning a South Branch cruise, to make it on a weekend.

To add to our difficulties, water is now being pumped out of the river into Round Valley Reservoir at Hampton. Those

The old mill at Neshanic Station is fast disintegrating and like most such buildings is being vandalized. The dam makes a difficult carry on either side

93

Tucca-Ramma-Hacking, the meeting place of the waters, where the North and South Branches meet to form the Raritan

pumps are now stopped on weekends so the situation is now near normal for cruising canoeists and the fishermen.

At Clinton there are two old gristmills; the one on the left bank is over two hundred years old. During the early days of this country such mills could be found every few miles on this river.

From Clinton down to Hamden the river is very attractive. Never more than a few feet deep, it twists and turns through the lovely meadowland so typical of Hunterdon County. At Hamden the explorer will suddenly come upon a tiny hamlet of the sort to delight the artist and the antiquarian. The quiet river and milldam, the raceway and the gate above it, and the charming homes on the river shore, make a setting very much like many we have loved in Vermont.

Below Hamden the hills begin to crowd the stream again and the pace becomes a bit more hurried. On the right bank the high cliffs of traprock and shale, covered for quite a distance with a heavy growth of spruce and hemlock, present a

The nineteenth-century iron bridge over the river at Neshanic Station is an example of the fast disappearing bridges of this type in New Jersey

totally new picture. The country through here is less accessible by road and thus it has retained a greater degree of wild natural beauty. Mile after mile of the same sort of scenery greets the explorer, all the way to Flemington Junction. A short carry around the dam at the junction and two more milldams below are easy to negotiate and they serve to make one pause long enough to admire the beauty of the scene.

From Flemington Junction all the way to the mouth of the river the canoeing is good most of the season. There are some shallows, but not enough to interfere seriously with the cruiser. The many milldams help to back up the water in sufficient volume to enable one to cruise without too much wading. The earliest gristmills in the state were along here.

Many old New Jersey towns are passed in the journey downriver from Flemington Junction—Three Bridges, Woodfern, Neshanic, and South Branch are among them. It is easy to follow the river by car or on foot as good roads are close to the stream all the way.

Those who have known the river for many years will recall the lovely old covered bridge which spanned the stream at South Branch. It suffered the fate of many others a few years ago, when it was replaced by a modern concrete bridge. On the right bank of the river, just above the bridge, stood a village blacksmith shop.

The South Branch is joined by the North Branch at a place known to the Indians as Tucca-Ramma-Hacking or "the meeting place of the waters." From this point to Raritan Bay the stream is officially the Raritan River. Since the original publication of this book in 1942 the old dam, just below the junction of the North and the South Branch, has been washed out. A new dam has been built and the old canal, extending from above the dam to the Raritan, will again be filled with water and usable for canoeing.

Just below the dam at Tucca-Ramma-Hacking, on the

At the Boating Pavillion in Duke Island Park refreshments are for sale
and canoes and rowboats may be rented for use on the old water-power
canal. Private canoes may not be used on the canal

left shore of the river, is Duke Island Park. This beautifully
situated unit of the Somerset County Park System, covering
an area of 250 acres between the river and the Old York
Road, was the gift of Miss Doris Duke, daughter of the late
James B. Duke.

Through the middle of the Park runs the old canal that
supplied water for the turbines that operated the original
textile mills in Raritan and later for power and light for the
Duke estate, across the Raritan River. The boating pavilion
is located on the canal and canoes and rowboats are rented
there for use on a limited area of it. Privately owned canoes
are not permitted.

Duke Island Park is very popular with family groups.
It has a band amphitheater shell in which music events, plays
and other programs are held in the summer. Tennis, fishing
and a myriad of children's play devices and plenty of shade
for picnicking or just loafing are also major attractions of
the Park.

THE NORTH BRANCH

The North Branch, unlike the South Branch, really appears to be a branch and not a part of the Raritan River. The rugged hill country of Morris County in which the North Branch has its beginning in a swamp that until a few years ago was a mill pond supplying water for the gristmill at Ralston, has more of a "sharp valley" or closed-in appearance.

This stream offers a great deal of interest for both those who may want to explore it by car and the canoeist who may want to paddle downstream. The car explorer should start at the hamlet of Ralston on Highway 24 between Chester and Mendham. Here one may visit the local historical museum which is in the building that for many years was the Post Office for Ralston. In fact, it was the oldest continuously operated Post Office in the State of New Jersey. From there follow the stream down through Peapack-Gladstone to Far Hills on Highway 512. From that point continue through Bedminster on Route 202 and the River Road to the village of North Branch. The end of the North Branch is not far below.

The canoeist should begin cruising from a point about a mile south of Bedminster and plan to take out at either Burnt Mills, for a short cruise, or at the mouth of the river where it joins the South Branch to form the Raritan.

The area around Peapack and Gladstone, in the upper river valley, is of great historic interest and on some of the surrounding hills are many elegant estates that are now occupied mainly by caretaker staffs.

On the main street of Peapack may be seen the ruins of one of the earliest lime-burning kilns in New Jersey. During the late years of the eighteenth century, lime produced here was tried as an experiment on local farms to sweeten the soil

THE INDIAN TRAIL
FROM THE DELAWARE AT MINISINK
TO THE SEA AT NAVESINK PASSED
THROUGH THE RAVINE NEARBY
IN THIS VICINITY BEFORE 1680
WAS THE CABIN OF
CORNELIS VAN LANGEVELDT
(CORNELIUS LONGFIELD)
FIRST SETTLER OF NEW BRUNSWICK
ON THIS LAND
HESSIAN GRENADIERS HAD THEIR
CAMP AND A REDOUBT
WHEN GENERAL HOWE AND
THE BRITISH ARMY OCCUPIED
THE CITY DECEMBER 1, 1776
TO JUNE 22, 1777

The Minisink Indian Path. On the east side of George Street, near the Douglass College Center, this glacial boulder marks the route of the most notable of the New Jersey Indian paths. Beginning at Minisink Island in the upper Delaware River it extends southeastward through New Brunswick to Navesink on the ocean. It crosses another of the New Jersey paths, the Assunpink Trail, further up the Raritan River

99

It is early spring and this view near the source of the river gives promise
of an early start of the canoe cruising season

Logan's Mill at the source of the river in Ralston. A small pond earlier furnished the head of water to operate the mill. The building is now a private residence

and increase crop yield. The experiments were so successful that lime came into general use on farms elsewhere.

The canoeist will find that it is not practical to consider cruising the North Branch from a point above Bedminster, unless a fast run is planned during periods of high waters. Under such conditions a start may be made several miles above Route 202.

We class this stream as a spring cruise and under normal water conditions the best place to start is about a mile below Bedminster where an easy portage across the meadow from Route 202 is possible.

During a cruise last May, when the water level should have normally been sufficient to paddle without too much wading, we were out of the canoe as much as in it, most of the first few miles below our starting point.

One of the oldest standing former post offices in New Jersey is on Highway 24 at Ralston. The building, erected in 1775, is now the headquarters and museum of the Ralston Historical Association

Due to the realignment of local roads in the construction of the new Highways 78 and 287, it is now difficult to follow the upper river by car to determine the place to leave a car for a return to the place where the trip begins. A free map that may be obtained from the Somerset County Park Commission, Somerville, N.J., will prove helpful in making plans for canoeing on the North Branch.

Below the suggested starting place the river sweeps around a wide bend, with high shale cliffs along the left shore. A short distance below the cliffs it passes under the old highway and under the new Interstate Highway 287. After that the evidences of modern civilization are not much of an intrusion. The river continues through beautiful meadowland with the fields a riot of color of bluebells and other spring wildflowers. Soon a low dam blocks the stream. Ordinarily this would

Beginning of a canoe trip on the North Branch from Bedminster to Burnt Mills

The old lime kiln on Main Street in Peapack. This is one of the earliest and here was burned the lime first used in the valley for farm purposes

Occasionally, on a fast shallow stream like the North Branch, a tricky combination of a dam with rock-strewn water below it makes a difficult carry

That section of the South Branch west of Highway 202 from Flemington Junction is a beautifully shaded section of the river for canoeing on a summer day

The beautiful tree-covered shale cliffs below the Highway 78 bridge

Paddling past the forested shale cliffs on a part of the river deep enough for the effective use of paddles

not present much of a problem to either carry around or to drop the canoe on a line over it to the water below. However, because of the fast, rock-strewn water below it is necessary to lift the canoe over from the center and, on a long line, let it drift through the broken water to one of the canoe party below.

For a cruise of a half day or less the road at Burnt Mills, just above the point where the Lamington River enters, is a good take-out place. From that point, if a car has been left there, it is only a fifteen minute drive back to the starting place to get the other car.

In the area west of Pluckemin the absence of fences is noticeable. That is the famous fox-hunt country of Somerset County where meets are regularly held in season.

Below the Lamington River the water is deeper and involves less wading until the low dam above Highway 22 is reached. Above the highway for nearly a mile along the

Old Queens, now the administration building of Rutgers University, was built between 1809 and 1811. A continental artillery unit commanded by Colonel Alexander Hamilton shelled the British across the Raritan River from a position near here during the retreat across the Jerseys

The Van Vechten House on the river bank above the bridge at Finderne. It was built by Michael Van Vechten in 1700, and was the headquarters of General Nathanael Greene during the occupation of Camp Middlebrook

river is North Branch Park, a part of the Somerset County park system. Picnicking is permitted there and Scout camporees are sometimes allowed but overnight camping is not permitted as far as we know.

From Highway 22 down to the mouth of the North Branch, where it meets the South Branch and forms the Raritan, the water is shallow, dropping over many shale ledges and making it difficult to paddle.

If and when the huge contemplated Confluence Reservoir

is built, it will provide deep water up the North and South Branches for several miles and west along the Old York Road toward Readington. Canoeing will then be much better in this area. The plan also calls for water to be piped from the upper Delaware River to the source of both the South and the North Branches to permit the release of more water, when needed, and thus maintain proper levels at all times.

We were recently thoroughly briefed on all projected reservoir plans for the entire state by Robert L. Hardman, chief engineer of the Division of Water Policy and Supply, and his associate, Donald J. Koeck. Such a briefing will convince anyone that those plans should be implemented as soon as possible to provide the water needed for human consumption and for the maintenance of proper flow to prevent stagnation and further pollution.

Rutgers University boathouse below the end of the Canal and former outlet lock. The city of New Brunswick is in the background and the Raritan River on the right

The Passaic

This slow-moving, roving stream, the second longest river in New Jersey, has its source in the tangled morass of the Great Swamp, remnant of ancient Lake Passaic. It is over eighty-five miles from the headwaters of the Passaic to Newark Bay, into which it drains. The river passes through or borders seven counties. It is a river of great diversity of terrain and is subject to flood conditions which often cause it to leave the normal channels and spread over the adjoining countryside for miles.

The last glacier to cover the northern part of the State, the Wisconsin Ice Sheet, reached the Paterson-Little Falls area on its way south about fifteen thousand years ago. It was several thousand years before it advanced to its southern terminus at what is now Basking Ridge. For many thousands of years the valley of the Passaic, from Paterson to Moggy Hollow, was filled with ice several thousand feet in depth.

When the ice began to melt and the glacier to recede, Lake Passaic was formed. It was a body of water over thirty miles long and from eight to twelve miles wide. Before the erosion through Moggy Hollow and through what is now the Millington Ravine began, the lake was in places nearly two hundred feet deep.

An interesting geologic fact about the ancient lake, and the glacier that caused it, is that in its retreat the gap in the first Watchung Mountain at what is now Short Hills was sealed with debris, changing the course of the Hudson River that had previously flowed through it.

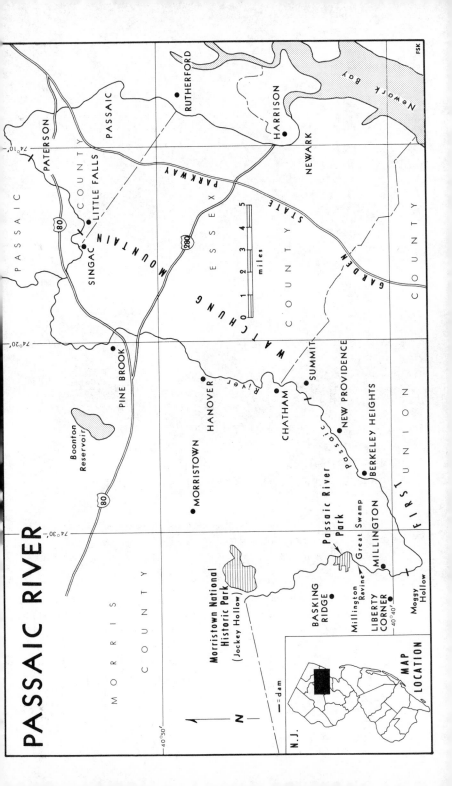

PASSAIC RIVER

N

MORRIS COUNTY

Boonton Reservoir

Morristown National Historic Park (Jockey Hollow)

BASKING RIDGE

= dam

N.J.

MAP LOCATION

40°50'

74°30'

PINE BROOK

MORRISTOWN

HANOVER

Passaic River Park

Millington Ravine

Great Swamp

LIBERTY CORNER

MILLINGTON

Maggy Hollow

40°40'

74°20'

PASSAIC

PASSAIC COUNTY

SINGAC

LITTLE FALLS

80

PATERSON

74°10'

WATCHUNG MOUNTAIN

280

CHATHAM

Passaic River

SUMMIT

NEW PROVIDENCE

BERKELEY HEIGHTS

ESSEX COUNTY

PARKWAY

STATE

GARDEN

RUTHERFORD

HARRISON

NEWARK

Newark Bay

UNION COUNTY

FIRST

miles

0 1 2 3 4 5

FSK

When the Wisconsin Ice Sheet retreated to the north it created Lake
Passaic with a water depth of over 200 feet. While it was draining
through Moggy Hollow, erosion was cutting narrow Millington Gorge
which permitted further drainage through the new outlet following the
channel of the present Passaic River. The Millington Gorge is today a
beautiful mountain ravine with hemlock covered banks

The Great Swamp, remnant of ancient Lake Passaic, is now a National Wildlife Refuge, administered by the U.S. Department of the Interior. Shown here is the source of the Passaic River west of Stirling Road

Over a long period of time the lake gradually drained away, primarily through Moggy Hollow near Liberty Corner, as it is now, and through the Millington Ravine to the present channel of the Passaic River.

Today the actual remnants of that ancient lake may be seen at three places along the Passaic River. They are the Great Swamp, a Federal Wildlife Refuge near Basking Ridge, the Hatfield Swamp at Hanover, and the Great Piece Meadows farther downstream. Those swamps are the only evidences of that once great body of glacial melt known as Lake Passaic that remain today.

In the course of a single day of exploration on this river, mile after mile of well-ordered and cultivated farms are passed and then, without warning, areas of tangled swamp-

This part of the river below the Millington Ravine, just above Valley Road, is a good place to begin a cruise down the Passaic

land and marshes close in on the stream. It becomes a modern wilderness in the midst of densely populated north Jersey. In the swamps and marshes a total of one hundred different species of birds have been seen and identified in a single day. Deer are plentiful and, until recent years, an occasional bear was shot in the interior of the Great Swamp. The migrating ducks and geese use the Passaic and its marshes to rest on their long migrations north and south.

During the spring it is possible to paddle a canoe on any part of the river, but for ordinary conditions it is best to start such journeys at the bridge south of Millington. From that point one may paddle all the way to Singac.

Flowing in a southeasterly direction, then breaking through a range of hills at Basking Ridge, the river hurries through a mile-long ravine, striking the valley at Millington. The early settlers took full advantage of this fast water and built their gristmills below the ravine. Shallow water is the rule until the highway bridge is reached, but below that point there is plenty of water for cruising in all but the driest seasons. Along both shores is the typical meadowland with plenty of oak forest near the river.

Some idea of the manner in which the Passaic wanders in its course may be realized from the fact that while one may drive a car from Millington to Summit in a few minutes it takes a full day of paddling to reach the same point by canoe. It loops and turns continuously and in fact flows in every direction somewhere during its journey. It is pleasant canoeing water as few settlements intrude upon it until Chatham is reached. In former years a great deal of canoeing was done on this part of the Passaic.

For many years, beyond the memory of the oldest inhabitants of the Passaic Valley, disastrous floods have each spring swept down the river and caused millions of dollars' damage

to property and sometimes loss of life. The New Jersey
Flood Control Commission and the Corps of Army Engineers
have tried, with little success to date, to develop some method
for controlling the rampaging waters. As the flood waters
overflow into the vast expanse of meadowlands they also
bring on a mosquito problem.

Some thirty years ago a plan was considered and widely
publicized that was hoped to be the answer to the flood
problem. It called for the virtual re-creation of ancient glacial
Lake Passaic. It was believed that such a huge, man-made
lake would check and hold the flood waters for gradual

The Basking Ridge Presbyterian Church, built in 1840 on the site of an
earlier church building, erected about 1710. The oak tree at the right is
reputed to be three hundred years old

Below New Providence for most of the way to Chatham the shores are higher and more heavily wooded. This is the view from below New Providence

release downstream. Even at that time, however, before the great increase in housing and industry, the estimated cost was staggering. Today the cost of the land and the building of the reservoir would be astronomical.

Various agencies, county, state and federal, are still trying to work out some practical plan to control the pollution in the lower river which is fast reaching a point of no return. Perhaps in the solution of the pollution problem the method of controlling the floods will be developed as well.

While the Passaic is not beautiful, in the sense that the Great Egg Harbor, the Rancocas, the Millstone, and other New Jersey rivers are, it has a charm of its own. It is the beauty of the silent and mysterious swampland, and it offers many unusual photographic opportunities for those who like to record their journeys on film.

There are a few down trees in the course of the river to Summit but beyond that point it is free of obstructions for the remaining thirty-five miles to Little Falls.

In this lovely old church, not far from the river, according to tradition, a balcony collapsed in 1838 and the village was renamed New Providence in thankfulness that no one was injured

118

At Pine Brook the Whippany River enters from the left. During the early days of the state this tributary stream was known to the Indians as the Whippanong, and it was along its shores that they made their homes. All through this part of the Passaic it winds and twists to such an extent that four miles of travel by water is necessary to cover a mile by land. The current is so slow that it is hardly noticeable and one may paddle up- or downstream without much effort.

Following a northerly course for another dozen miles, the river then turns to the east, near Towaco, beyond which the Ramapo River adds its volume of water to the Passaic. From here to Singac the river is much wider and deeper. The surrounding countryside is more settled, and permanent homes and summer camps line the shores. The sport of canoeing was in its glory on this part of the stream years ago and there were literally thousands of privately owned and rental canoes to be seen on any Saturday or Sunday. This local canoeing was quite different from that of the typical cruiser. It was the weekend, radio, lazy-paddling sort of thing.

A mile below Singac is Little Falls and the end of practical canoeing on this river. High natural falls hemmed in with industrial plants make the portages extremely difficult and it should not be attempted. The Morris Canal crossed here on a high, arched aqueduct of stone. Nothing remains of it today.

After its drop over the falls and a short run through the gorge below, the Passaic slows its pace again and from that point to the falls at Paterson it becomes a slow-moving stream of considerable depth in places. The various communities and the county have developed both shores into a continuous park, ending in Paterson's attractive West Side Park. It was below the site of the park, just above the bridge which crosses the

It is generally believed that like the conditions found below Little Falls in the Passaic, the entire river is fouled up with debris and heavily polluted. This view taken near Stirling, on the upper river, clearly indicates that this is not so

river, that John P. Holland launched his first submarine in May 1881. This crude one-man craft successfully submerged and was propelled both under and on the waters of the Passaic, and it now proudly rests in the Paterson Museum. In the park stands one of the earliest of the commercially successful submarines as a monument to Holland.

At one time canoeing was very popular with local people. We were told that private canoe clubs were very numerous between Passaic and Little Falls. Today one may hire rowboats and motorboats but we failed to find any canoes along this part of the river.

Below the river bridge the Great Falls of Paterson tumble over a traprock precipice a hundred feet in height. This is an impressive sight during the spring floods and in winter when the fall is a mass of ice.

The Great Falls at Paterson that were the inspiration for Alexander
Hamilton's "The Society for Establishing Useful Manufactures" in 1791.
The textile mills built there were a part of the first organized manufactur-
ing efforts in America

The hand-made sheet-metal submarine is the experimental craft invented by John Holland and tested in the nearby Passaic River in 1878. It may be seen in the Paterson Museum daily from 1 to 5 P.M. Admission is free

Paterson and the river passing near it are intimately associated with an historic enterprise that has become symbolic of American industry. In 1791 an organization was formed under the leadership of Alexander Hamilton, known as The Society for Establishing Useful Manufactures. Legislation was granted to permit its functioning. A mile-square area was designated, embracing much of what is now the city of Paterson, and purchased by the newly organized company. The plans were centered on the water power available in the falls and a cotton mill was the first venture. Other budding industries were invited to join the group but, as in so many ambitious plans of this kind, bickering among the organizers soon disrupted the original plans. However, plants were built independently and the present city of Paterson is the result.

Years ago the lower part of the river was known as one of the most attractive streams in the eastern part of the country. The Jersey sandstone Dutch Colonial homes of the early settlers, surrounded by well-kept yards extending down to the shores of the river, made an attractive picture. Boat clubs were numerous and some of the most famous scullers of another generation were developed on the river. Along the river road between Newark and Rutherford were large estates, similar to many in the Virginia tidewater area.

With the advent of industrial activity, quick to take advantage of the plentiful supply of pure water and the unexcelled shipping facilities to the ports of the world, the charm and beauty of the ancient Passaic disappeared.

Ten years ago when we re-checked the rivers in connection with the first revised edition of this book, we expressed hope that the lower Passaic River would be cleared of the old ship hulks and other debris. At that time communities like Belleville, Nutley, and others, with the help of some industries bordering the river, started a clean-up job that did result in the removal of some of the old hulks and the creation of some riverside parks. However, during the intervening years the great increase in industry and housing and the inadequate sewage treatment facilities have made the pollution a far greater problem. The lower Passaic is now listed as one of the most polluted rivers in America. A staff article in the *Newark Evening News* recently characterized it as "Sad, Silted, Smelly."

That is why we no longer consider the river a canoeing stream below Little Falls.

The Ramapo

The country surrounding the Ramapo River is more rugged than that through which most New Jersey rivers flow. The main branch starts as the outlet of a small pond just east of Highway 17, near Tuxedo Park. For several miles, it takes on more of the appearance of a wilderness stream. The majestic forests form an appropriate background for the river, and in turn the river adds to the beauty of that great recreational park, as the singing waters flow along.

There is not sufficient water for cruising above Suffern except during spring floods and in fact much of this part of the stream to a point below Suffern has lost its original charm, because of commercial development.

For a great many years the members of the Atlantic Division of the American Canoe Association, the sponsor of organized canoeing in America, have made an annual event of a spring weekend cruise on this river, starting at Tuxedo. During the season of high water the upper stream sometimes taxes the ability of even the expert canoeist. The high banks confine the full flood, and the boulders and other obstructions create white-water conditions that cause an occasional upset and a swim to shore.

There is something about such a group cruise that is difficult to describe. The good fellowship of thirty or forty men and women, all keenly interested in the sport; the frequent upsets, rescues, and the sharing of dry clothing; the end of the day and the evening campfire and songs—all are

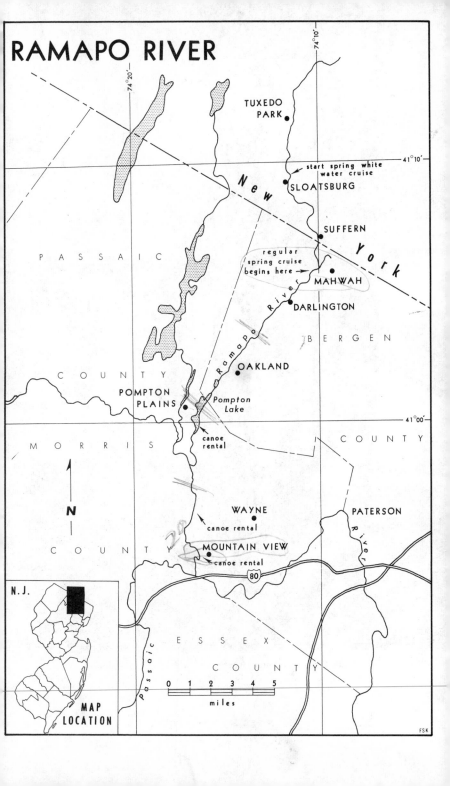

RAMAPO RIVER

74°20'

74°10'

TUXEDO PARK

41°10'

New

start spring white water cruise

SLOATSBURG

York

SUFFERN

P A S S A I C

regular spring cruise begins here →

MAHWAH

River

DARLINGTON

B E R G E N

Ramapo

C O U N T Y

OAKLAND

POMPTON PLAINS

Pompton Lake

41°00'

canoe rental

M O R R I S

C O U N T Y

N

C O U N T Y

WAYNE

canoe rental

PATERSON

River

MOUNTAIN VIEW

canoe rental

80

N.J.

MAP LOCATION

Passaic

E S S E X

C O U N T Y

0 1 2 3 4 5

miles

FSK

The high dam at Pompton where most weekend canoe cruises end

things to be remembered, to be treasured always. It is that indescribable something that has kept alive such an organization as the American Canoe Association through ninety years or more. Men of seventy are still active in the affairs of that group.

Carrying on the tradition, the Murray Hill Canoe Club and other groups still schedule spring cruises on the Ramapo River. In mid-April last year the authors joined the Murray Hill Club for a cruise that was to begin below Mahwah, off Route 202. Upon our arrival at nine o'clock we found some of the members alternately preparing their canoes for the trip and blowing on their hands in the near-freezing temperature.

We had to forego the pleasure of accompanying the group by canoe. Instead we spent some time photographing the preparations and, after seeing them disappear around a bend in the river, we had some hot coffee and then followed in our car along Route 202.

As is usual, at the beginning of many cruises, one of the men, attempting to dodge trees and brush in a bit of fast water, rolled over in the cold water. However, it was a beautiful sunny day and the canoeist who had an upset didn't seem to mind his misadventure. Joining the group at their lunch break in the lee of an old bridge, we learned there had been more upsets on the way downstream. By swapping dry clothes around among those who had received a dunking the incidents seemed of little account.

The high enthusiasm of this genial group of people reminded us that in our many years of outdoor activities we have always found canoeists and campers to be happy people, thoroughly enjoying group activities like this cruise. For those interested in such events we suggest joining one of the many canoe clubs that are active throughout New Jersey.

The authors at the Mahwah rendezvous at the start of the Murray Hill
Canoe Club cruise in April 1970. (Al Hanna photo)

For a wider range of canoeing and camping such as the
annual encampments of the American Canoe Association, one
may join that organization, the membership of which is open
to both men and women.

As a part of our photographic coverage for the Ramapo
trip we drove downstream, looking for a high bluff from
which we could get some pictures of the fleet, through the
trees, on their way downstream. One of the pictures in this
chapter gives an example of what we were trying to say with
our camera, about this event, when the trees are still bare of
foliage, the air crisp, and the thrill of the first canoe trip in
the spring.

Parallel with the river all the way to Pompton Lake, the
beautiful and somewhat mysterious Ramapo Mountains loom
up. Those aged hills have always retained their wild and for-

bidding aspect and few roads or trails cross them. Rattlesnakes are found in abundance in them, and some of the people who have lived in the fastness of the hills for generations are practically without contact with the civilized world. It may seem strange, but there are places in the Ramapo hills where the natives live in a state comparable to conditions in sections of Appalacia.

A mile or so above Oakland the Ramapo enters a valley with the mountains crowding down to the very shores of the

Members of the Murray Hill Canoe Club preparing to start a spring cruise on the Ramapo from Mahwah to Oakland. It was early in April, air and water temperature not much above freezing. Brilliant sunshine tempered the cold as the cruise got under way. Such is the enthusiasm of the ardent canoeist

Sometimes this river can be tricky during the spring. A Murray Hill Canoe Club member shows good form in this bit of fast water

stream. Musical little rapids add to the other sounds of nature as the traveler by canoe journeys along. The motorist who drives along Route 202 misses the charm of that part of Oakland which is on the river. From the village downstream to the dam above Pompton Lake the river is very popular with fishermen and afternoon and evening paddlers. It is easy to understand why the Indians loved this spot so much.

During the spring runs an added fillip is given to the sport in the attempts to drop over the low dams encountered on the way. It is a feat that seems easy and perfectly logical to save a carry but too often it turns out to be a sport for the onlooker alone. Upsets are frequent, and in early April, with the water temperature near freezing, such a mishap requires some hardihood for the venturesome canoeist.

After leaving the dam below Oakland the river soon begins to widen out into Pompton Lake. For a mile or so the shores are bordered with rushes and soon one emerges into the lake

Part of the fleet of the Murray Hill Canoe Club as they pass below the high bluff near Darlington

Getting ready to resume the cruise following a lunch break in the meadow at Darlington

A pleasant vista on the river where it widens out into Pompton Lake above
the dam

proper. This lake was built through the damming of the river at the village of Pompton to generate power, but it is as attractive as many of our northern natural lakes. Cottages line both shores and on the west side are recreational places, boat liveries, and the like. It is also popular in the winter during the skating season. On the high wooded eastern shore is Sunnybank, the home of the late Albert Payson Terhune, who was known and loved all over the world for his dog stories.

While the present village of Pompton has the appearance of other typical New Jersey towns, it retains much of its historic atmosphere. The first homes were built about 1682 and the neighborhood was settled largely by the Dutch. It was noted for its early iron furnaces.

Below Pompton Lake the river becomes deeper and wider and no difficulty will be experienced in paddling from there to the mouth of the stream. It becomes more winding and is flanked by lovely homes. It is ideal for paddling and is used extensively by canoeists. From here on, the river is actually the Pompton, although it is still indicated as the Ramapo on the road maps. At a point near Pompton Plains another branch enters from the right. This branch is an outlet of the famous Wanaque Reservoir.

It is an easy matter to hire a canoe at Wayne or other nearby canoe rental places, then drive on a few miles to Pompton with the canoe on the top of the car, and, after a pleasant day on the water, carry the canoe back to the rental place. For a longer trip one may paddle from Pompton to the end of the river where it joins the Passaic, and then paddle up the Passaic as far as time permits. The return trip can then be made down the Passaic again to Singac. Transportation back to the point where you left your car can be arranged at a local garage in the village of Singac.

The Paulins Kill

The land through which the Paulins Kill flows presents a bold and picturesque outline. The Kittatinny Mountain Range parallels the entire course of the river, the rugged hills actually extending to its very shores. The river turns and twists around the many hills as it hurries along to the Delaware. The Indians named this lovely mountain stream "Tockhockonetkong" and to them the mountains were "Kittatinny" or "chief town," for it was from the shores of the river, protected on the west by the mountain range, that the chiefs of the Lenni Lenapes governed their people.

There is an interesting story about the origin of the present name of the stream. Following the battle of Trenton, some of the Hessian prisoners were taken to the village of Stillwater and there they were held until the end of the war. Many of them liked the country so much that they bought land and settled permanently. One of them became a prominent man in the affairs of the valley and the river was named in honor of his daughter Pauline. Many of the present-day residents of the Paulins Kill valley trace their ancestry back to those Hessian prisoners of war who made this the country of their adoption.

If you will look at a map of Sussex and Warren counties, in the extreme northwestern part of the state, you will see how clearly the mountains separate the valley of the Delaware from the Paulins Kill. When viewing these rugged hills from the Delaware Valley it seems as if some volcanic upheaval

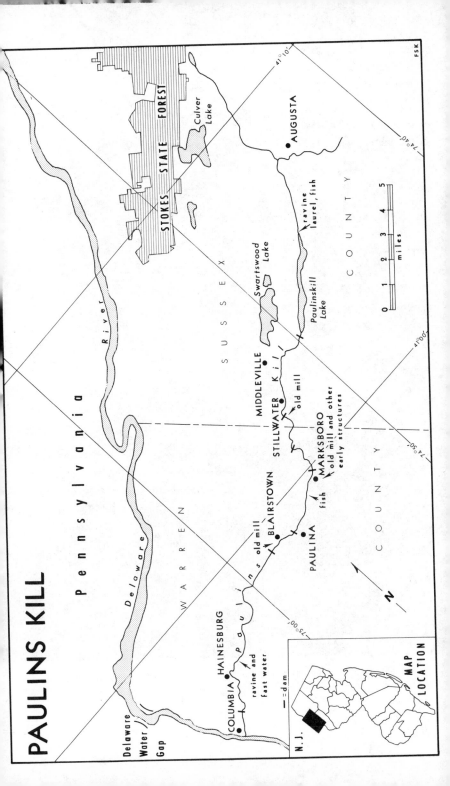

PAULINS KILL

Pennsylvania

Delaware River

Delaware Water Gap

STOKES STATE FOREST

Culver Lake

AUGUSTA

ravine, laurel, fish

COUNTY

Swartswood Lake

SUSSEX

Paulinskill Lake

MIDDLEVILLE

Stillwater Kill

old mill

MARKSBORO
old mill and other
early structures

BLAIRSTOWN

old mill

fish

fish

PAULINA

WARREN

HAINESBURG

Paulins Kill

ravine and
fast water

COLUMBIA

COUNTY

N

— = dam

0 1 2 3 4 5
miles

N.J.

MAP
LOCATION

FSK

41°10'

74°40'

41°00'

74°50'

75°00'

The mill with the tail-race from the river in the foreground as it appears today in the quiet little village of Swiftwater

must have split the earth along what is now the Delaware River, and thus turned it over into these two New Jersey counties, to form the western barrier to this corner of our state. They rise to an elevation of over 1,800 feet at High Point, and approximately half of their length has been taken over for state parks. We may now enjoy unsurpassed mountain scenery and recreational facilities in the Stokes State Forest and at High Point Park.

The oldest road of any considerable length in the United States follows the east shore of the Delaware. It is the Old Mine Road, built by the Dutch in the seventeenth century, from Kingston, N.Y., to the Indian copper mines at Pahaquarry, just north of Columbia. Copper was transported by oxcart to Kingston and then shipped to Holland. Much of the road remains today in the same condition as it was during its early days. In fact it is possible to drive or walk from Columbia to a point near Port Jervis over the ancient road. Beyond that place it becomes lost in the network of modern highways. If the Tocks Island Reservoir and recreational development are completed, and at this time the enthusiasm for its completion seems to be diminishing, all of the Old Mine Road from the planned earthen dam at the Delaware Water Gap to Port Jervis will be under water.

Let us climb our rugged Kittatinnies again and go back to the valley of the Paulins Kill. The actual beginning of this river is at a point near Augusta, and for the first few miles it is not much more than a mountain brook. A mile or so below, the water is backed up by an old dam and from there the stream cascades from rock to rock in its quick passage through the many little ravines. The wildest scenery and the fastest water may be found in the few miles from Augusta to Paulins Kill. A few miles below Halsey the river slows down and for the next five miles becomes Paulins Kill Lake,

Springhouses built of native Jersey sandstone with a spring running through them to keep milk and meat cool are becoming rare in our countryside. This one, built in the middle eighteenth century, is near Augusta

which is paralleled on both sides by hills and meadows, making it a very attractive boating and fishing area. In early years there was a series of small ponds, each with its wood dam and gristmill. Today one may spend a pleasant afternoon canoeing and fishing along its shores.

It is difficult to explore the upper part of the river, except for an occasional place accessible from the narrow mountain roads. The canoeist does not find it any easier, as it is not possible even to paddle on this part of the stream except during the high water, and then the rocks and falls make such a trip inadvisable. In fact, cruising on the Paulins Kill should be confined to the water between Stillwater and Columbia, and should be planned for spring when the run-off from the winter snows provides an extra foot of water. It is possible to paddle on some parts of the river at any time, but higher than normal water is required for a continuous trip.

When cruising this stream in flood some caution is necessary. The conditions below the dam at Marksboro and at Hainesburg should be examined carefully. Considerable skill with a paddle is required at some stages of the high water.

For those who may want to explore the Paulins Kill by car we would advise driving directly from Newton to the foot of Paulins Kill Lake and then continuing downstream via Middleville, Stillwater, Marksboro, Hainesburg, and Columbia. Good roads follow the entire stream.

An excellent large-scale map of Sussex County may be obtained free by writing the Board of Chosen Freeholders, Administration Building, Newton, N.J. The brochure and

An attractive long and narrow lake created by the damming of the river east of Middleville. It is a favorite haunt of fishermen

map are full of interesting information about the county, which includes the upper half of the Paulins Kill. It will prove very helpful both for the canoeist and for those who would like to explore the river and the beautiful country through which it flows by car.

There is glorious scenery throughout the valley and there are many places of historic interest. At Stillwater, for example, the explorer will find a charming village which was the first settlement in the valley. Casper Shafer, a German immigrant, was one of the earliest of the settlers. He built the first crude gristmill and later added a sawmill here in 1750. The products of these mills were floated down the river on flatboats to the Delaware and thence to Philadelphia. As the lower

A quiet pastoral scene on the Paulins Kill near Hainesburg

Rock-filled fast water below the bridge at Hainesburg with the village in the background

valley became settled a great many power dams were built and it then became necessary to carry the flour and lumber overland in oxcarts.

Blairstown, the "gem of the Paulins Kill," is a pleasantly situated town with homes and business buildings clustered around the sides and tops of a series of rolling hills. The well-known Blair Academy is located here.

The old tailrace has been made into a park which, together with the little lake above it, provides a very pleasant retreat for summer days. The stone gristmill on the main street is now the town library, and it is an unusually fine example of stonework. While we were photographing it recently, a local resident pointed out that it is possible to find practically every letter of the alphabet in the combinations of the various mortar joints between the cut stones.

As the river swings around the bend in its approach to Hainesburg, it is flanked on both sides by high, sheer cliffs which confine the waters of the stream into a stretch of fast rapids. The mile or so through these hills provides some very enjoyable white-water sport for the experienced canoeist during spring floods. The beginner should look this water over very carefully from the shore before attempting to navigate a canoe through the upper and lower rapid. The first run is fast but without many rocks or other obstructions, but the lower drop can be very dangerous.

Hainesburg as a settlement is not very old, although the stone gristmill on the south shore was built before the Revolution. On the side of the hill one may see some of the old stone lime kilns.

A lake of some size has been created through the building of a huge power dam above Columbia, and a short distance below the dam the waters of the Paulins Kill empty into the Delaware River. Just above that point one of the largest of the covered bridges ever built in eastern America spanned the Delaware River. It was replaced by a modern bridge many years ago. It was built to carry the lighter traffic of the horse era but it carried heavy motor traffic for years. The Old Mine Road begins near the New Jersey end of the present bridge.

At one time Columbia seemed destined to be a busy manufacturing town, as several attempts were made to establish a glassmaking center there. The glass forges were built in the middle of the last century and they passed from one owner to another, and finally they were abandoned. Today the village is quiet and peaceful, an excellent place to spend a restful vacation.

The Musconetcong

Except for an occasional mile or so here and there the Musconetcong is not a river that can be explored by canoe. Nevertheless, we consider it one of the most interesting rivers in New Jersey, with the wooded hills through which it passes and the few remnants of the old Morris Canal that remain. The canal is now practically gone but for many years during the nineteenth century it was the chief means of conveying coal, iron, and zinc across the northern part of the State to the Hudson River at Jersey City.

The river is the outlet of Lake Musconetcong and both the river and the lake were the principal sources of water to keep the Morris Canal filled. Therefore any story of the river would be incomplete if it did not include the story of the canal.

Until a few years ago it was possible to paddle a canoe on the canal from Stanhope west almost to Waterloo. Now most of it has been filled in through Stanhope and beyond. One of the streets of Stanhope bears the name Plane Street and is a reminder that at one time an inclined plane for lifting the canal barges was located there.

A wood barn used to stable the mules that hauled the maintenance boats when the canal was in operation may still be seen west of Stanhope. The river, which runs beside the canal from the lake, crosses over at this point and continues as a small stream to Waterloo, four miles to the west. It is

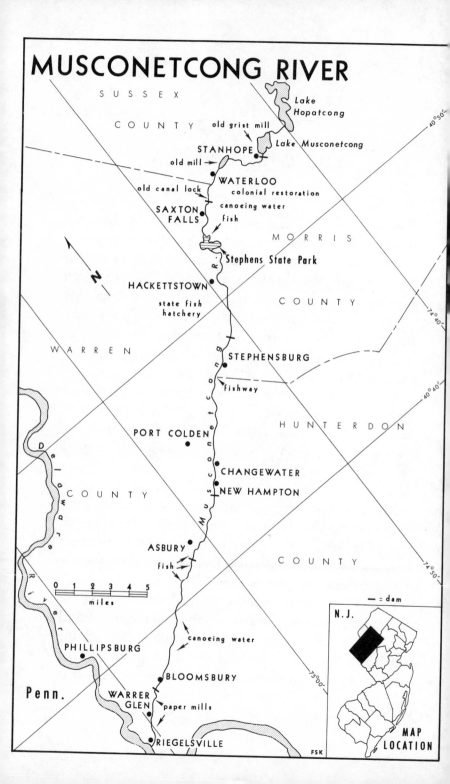

The Waterloo storehouse from which local farm products were loaded on canal barges for shipment on the Morris Canal. It is a part of the restoration of this interesting nineteenth-century village. On the first floor is the old general store

The north shore of Musconetcong Lake looking east from Highway 206. The lake is the headwaters of the Musconetcong River which is very popular as a center for summer and winter sports

possible to make the canal journey on foot, along the towpath. Smaller planes, plane houses, and other structures used on the canal will be seen along the way.

If driving, one should continue on Route 206 about two miles from Netcong, then turn left and follow the road into Waterloo.

Until a few years ago Waterloo, an eighteenth-century village that prospered from early iron mining operations and later the operation of the Morris Canal, very nearly became a ghost town in the hills. However, many people believed that the one-time charm and beauty of the historic landmark should be restored. As a result of the efforts and money spent on the restoration it appears today little changed from its earlier days and annually attracts thousands of visitors to see and enjoy the old storehouse and country store on the bank of the canal, the blacksmith shop, the old church, and the many other restored buildings now open to the public. Excellent musical programs are a part of the summer activities.

That part of the canal still intact that extends south from Waterloo toward Saxton Falls offers an opportunity for walks along the old towpath and one wouldn't be surprised to see a canal barge, towed by mules, come around the bend.

The big question is how long will we be able to enjoy Waterloo and its surroundings? The whole area of the Musconetcong Valley and river, including the restored village, will perhaps, by 1976, be buried under seventy feet of water, if the plans of the State of New Jersey to make it a

The old stone mill with the pond and water control gate above the tail-race

reservoir are carried out. This is just another penalty of the population explosion and the ever-growing need for more water.

Waterloo was founded by Peter Louis Smith and for many years it was the terminus of the Sussex Railroad of New Jersey. The road was built to carry zinc from Franklin Furnace and iron from Andover. This was loaded onto the canal boats in the basin through which the river flows, and then transported to Newark and Jersey City by canal.

Below Waterloo we find the river running beside the canal again, and at this point it widens out into more of a stream. However, there is seldom water enough to permit canoeing except during the spring floods. The hundreds of fishways and dams offer too many obstructions for easy cruising during

The Morris Canal as it appears today between Waterloo and Saxton Falls

Good luck and perhaps some skill on opening day may give you a catch
like this one, and then again perhaps not

normal height of water. Probably more work has been done
for fish propagation on this stream than on any other in
the state. Rock dams, fishways, traps, and other man-made
devices to provide good fishing waters have been installed
throughout the entire river. We commend this stream to the
disciples of Isaak Walton, who said:

> I care not, I, to fish in seas—
> Fresh rivers best my mind do please,
> Whose sweet calm course I contemplate,
> And seek in life to imitate.

A few miles below Waterloo is Saxton Falls, where the
river was dammed at the time of the building of the canal.
Control gates and lock may be seen near the dam. The lake
is a beautiful area of water, and one may paddle a canoe

The pool below Saxton Falls is annually the subject of statewide press coverage on the opening day of trout fishing. Usually a photograph is featured showing fishermen shoulder to shoulder around the pool

upstream for a mile or so. This is a favorite spot with trout fishermen, and the state has provided tables and fireplaces for their enjoyment. At Stephens State Park, too, a short distance below, may be found all necessary facilities for a day beside the river and very attractive stretches of water.

At Hackettstown one should plan to see the State Fish Hatchery. Trout, bass, and other fish are raised here to supply the lakes and streams of New Jersey. Some of the trout one may see in the pools are so large they seem unreal. Thirty-six-inch fish are not at all unusual—and that seems like a lot of fish to an angler who is accustomed to taking one or two ten-inch fish from the streams during the season.

Continuing along the river toward Washington, the road passes through Beattystown, which was a settlement before the Revolution. A few miles below at Stephensburg is a very interesting arched stone bridge with an intricate fishway below it.

Many old canal towns—Washington, Stewartsville, Port Colden, and others—remind one in many ways of the early canal days. Old timers still tell the stories that have somehow grown with the years. At Port Colden the route of the canal was directly west to the Delaware at Phillipsburg. One may still see the remains of the canal banks here and there along the road.

The river below Stephens-Saxton Falls State Park, showing one of the many State-constructed fishways to improve the trout fishing. Trout fishing is excellent in this part of the river and the stream is heavily stocked in season

At Asbury the Musconetcong begins to appear more like a navigable stream. It would be possible to paddle from there to the Delaware if there were not so many fish dams and weirs in the stream. Asbury is one of those exceedingly lovely little villages so common to North Jersey. It consists of a few dozen houses, a typically modern independent grocery store, the usual white country churches, and one industrial plant, a graphite factory. We love this little village and the rolling countryside surrounding it and have enjoyed many happy hours here during the bird-shooting season in November.

Below Asbury the river becomes more picturesque, but there is no road near enough to permit one to enjoy much of it by car until Bloomsbury is reached. The mile or so of the Musconetcong as it passes through that village is very attractive and because of the additional depth of water backed up by the mill dam it is used extensively for boating and fishing. Bloomsbury dates back to the stagecoach days when the present Route 22 was the old Easton Pike. In the village and surrounding countryside are many of the old and substantial stone houses of that earlier day.

From Warren Glen, a paper-making community, the river runs beside the road and continues to do so all the way to the Delaware River. Along the road are many old houses and a few of the early settlements—once busy places but now off the beaten track. The whole scene appears as something from the past, and many beautiful views unfold before the traveler as the river is followed. The photographer will be delighted with the subjects he finds as the Delaware and the end of our little river is reached.

The Toms

The swampy areas through which the upper part of this river passes, and the wild profusion of heavy brush on the banks of the stream, make the Toms River somewhat difficult to travel. We would not recommend it as a starter. However, the wild beauty and the clear cold water of the river more than compensate the cruiser for his effort. The motorist will find it difficult to get more than a glimpse of the upper twenty miles of the stream. The last ten miles, where the land is more open, and along the shores of the tidal estuary to Barnegat Bay, may be enjoyed from a car or on foot.

Like many of the smaller, winding streams of South Jersey, this river appears to be one which should be covered by canoe in a few hours' time. The actual mileage by water from Bowman's Mill bridge at Route 528 to Barnegat Bay is over thirty miles, or twice the distance by road.

The network of good roads, crossing the stream many times, enables one to start a canoe trip at any one of several places. Some parts of the stream, particularly from Whitesville, can be cruised during any season. For a trip from the headwaters at Holmeson one should check the water to make sure that it is possible to get through. The months of May and June are best, we find. The more temperate climate of this section makes it possible to travel this river in the late fall, after the seasonal rains.

While there are the usual number of small communities along the way, none of them is large enough or close enough

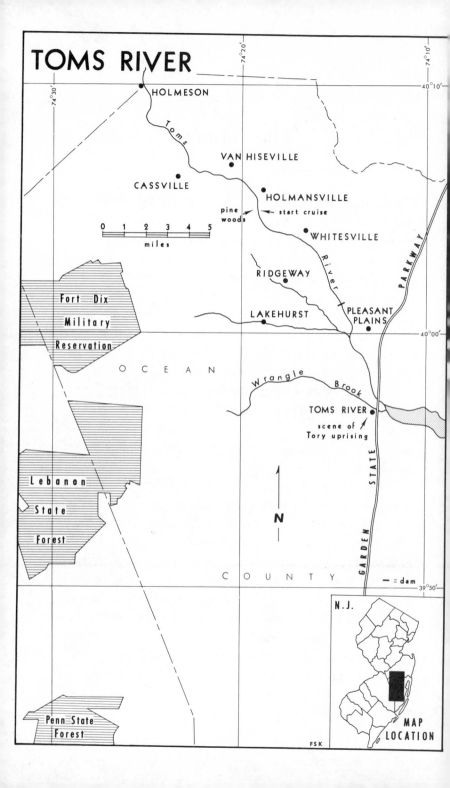

TOMS RIVER

74°30' 74°20' 74°10' 40°10'

HOLMESON

Toms

VAN HISEVILLE

CASSVILLE • HOLMANSVILLE

pine → ← start cruise
woods

WHITESVILLE

0 1 2 3 4 5
miles

RIDGEWAY

River

Fort Dix
Military
Reservation

LAKEHURST PLEASANT
PLAINS 40°00'

O C E A N

Wrangle Brook

TOMS RIVER

scene of ↑
Tory uprising

Lebanon

State

N

Forest

C O U N T Y

PARKWAY

GARDEN STATE

— = dam 39°50'

Penn State
Forest

N.J.

MAP
LOCATION

FSK

The river is narrow but possible to negotiate in a canoe in places like this, below the mill pond at Holmansville

Typical view of the pine-covered reaches of the Toms River in the heart of the southern section of the Pine Barrens. In this area the pines predominate instead of the white cedar of the Wharton State Forest area

Frequently burned-over areas of the Pine Barrens border much of the Toms, leaving acres of destroyed timber

The tall pines dominate the skyline on the lower Toms River where it opens up more than the upper part of the stream

to the river to enable one to get meals. It is best to carry provisions with you.

The upper ten miles of the Toms River run through typical swamp country which becomes flooded during periods of high water in the spring. During such times the river completely loses its identity and spreads out in every direction. It is difficult to determine the main channel, and unless the tree line is carefully watched the cruiser will find himself paddling into one of the many flooded areas without an outlet. When there is sufficient current it is possible to keep to the channel by letting the canoe drift along the faster water.

From Whitesville down to the Bay a totally different kind of country is encountered. Instead of the swampy shores found on the upper river, one will see firm, sandy soil covered with a heavy growth of oak and scrub pine. Through

157

Paint Island Spring, near the source of the Toms River, is a chalybeate spring containing a heavy concentration of supercarbonate of iron oxide in solution. The yellow solids in the bottom of the spring are commonly called ochre and it was used by the Indians to paint their faces for war

A rare artifact, a paint pot used by the Indians to hold the clays for painting their faces for war. It is shown in the palm of Thomas Brian of Kingston, its discoverer and owner

this area it is possible to go ashore and explore the surrounding country. For a weekend cruise one should plan to make the overnight camp below Whitesville. Not so many obstructions are encountered in this part of the stream. At times the river narrows down to a width of fifteen feet but it continues to run very fast and deep.

Below Route 70 the river opens up into a clear running stream with mile after mile of entrancing views quickly appearing around the bends. The shores are lined with a riot of all sorts of plant life. From here to Toms River it is hardly necessary to swing a paddle as the current pulls the canoe along. The Ridgeway Branch enters from the right at Pleasant Plains, and Wrangle Brook also joins the Toms.

Most voyagers on this stream end their journey at the dam above the village, as it is difficult to continue by canoe in the tidal water below the town of Toms River. At the bridge in the center of the village a canal-like stretch is used as a mooring basin for large pleasure boats, and beyond that is the tidal estuary extending seven miles to Barnegat Bay.

Toms River has a colorful history dating back beyond the War for Independence. The first buildings were a blockhouse, a few houses, and a mill. In 1782 a large group of Loyalists or Tories attacked the blockhouse defended by local patriots under Captain Joshua Huddy, who was forced to surrender when his supply of ammunition became exhausted. The Loyalists burned the fort and all other buildings in the town and hanged the valiant Captain Huddy at Gravelly Point. This act so enraged the people of the surrounding countryside that all Loyalists were forced to leave for more habitable parts until the end of the war.

In the center of Toms River formerly stood the Ocean House, built in 1787. This was for many years a well-known stagecoach tavern, noted for its hospitality. Like so many historic structures, it was torn down in the early sixties.

The Murray Hill Canoe Club and the Mohawk Canoe Club members spend a great deal of time keeping the river clear of brush and down timber from Whitesville to Toms River. On the annual schedule of cruises of both clubs special weekends are spent, not just enjoying cruising and camping on this interesting Pine Barrens stream. Instead on such weekends power saws, brush hooks and the like get as much of a work out as paddles.

This clearing work over the past three years has made possible a three-day cruise in normal height water from Whitesville instead of the two-day trip that was possible before the clearing projects began. It is a never-ending job as flood waters undercut and wash the dirt from the roots of the trees and they drop into the river.

October is a delightful time to cruise this river.

The Oswego River and Lake

During our explorations seeking material and photographs for the first edition of this book, which was published in 1942, we were familiar with the Wading River from Chatsworth to tidewater. The story of the wildness and unbelievable tangle of down timber we had to cut our way through was fully recounted at that time. A few years later we were invited to cruise what was then known as the Oswego Branch of the Wading River, by our good friends Mr. and Mrs. Malcom Runyon, and we became familiar with this lovely stream with its shores covered with heavy stands of white cedar. Since that first cruise we have paddled down from Oswego Lake to Harrisville many times. It is now our favorite canoeing water.

The source of the river lies above present-day Oswego Lake, a beautiful area of water extending over ninety acres. Feeding into it and bordering one shore of the lake flows the Oswego River. The lake is in the center of the thirty-three-thousand-acre Penn State Forest. Before the present causeway was built to create the larger and deeper lake it was a cranberry bog.

The lake, the swimming and picnicking facilities offer an opportunity to enjoy both a day of exploration around the lake and a swim before completing the day. If an overnight camp is planned, followed by a day of paddling down the river to Harrisville, a four-hour cruise, one may camp overnight on either shore of the river below the lake or at the

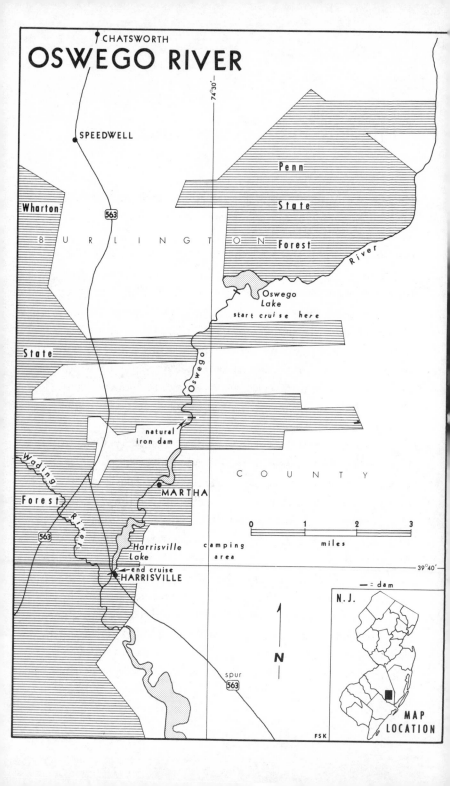

OSWEGO RIVER

CHATSWORTH

SPEEDWELL

Penn

State

Forest

Wharton

563

B   U   R   L   I   N   G   T   O   N

Oswego
Lake

start cruise here

River

State

Oswego

natural
iron dam

C   O   U   N   T   Y

MARTHA

0   1   2   3

miles

camping
area

Wading

River

Forest

563

Harrisville
Lake

39°40'

end cruise
HARRISVILLE

N

spur
563

— = dam

N.J.

MAP
LOCATION

FSK

74°30'

The Atlantic white cedars shown on the right are a part of a large stand
that borders the river

A group of Rutgers Outing Club women and even a baby about to start the day's run down from Oswego Lake to Harrisville

state campground at Harrisville, a part of the Wharton State Forest. A permit may be obtained from the local ranger or at the Bass River Park headquarters.

If you view with despair the ever-increasing pollution of our air and water, and the despoliation of our land, not to mention the almost total absence of clean water, take a day off, preferably a weekday, pick up a canoe from some rental place on the way and drive down to Penn State Forest, the wildest and most beautiful area of Burlington County, in the Pine Barrens.

Walk along the sandy shores of the lake and enjoy a rare sight, water so clean every pebble and grain of sand is clearly visible through the water. Farther out in the lake, where the water is deeper, it is a beautiful amber color from the cedar roots on the lake bottom. Believe it if you can, the entire lake is *clean* water and in fact it is claimed that it is actually potable.

After a leisurely paddle around the perimeter of the lake, enjoy a picnic lunch and perhaps a refreshing swim in the lake. Following lunch carry your canoe over the causeway below the lower end of the lake and start the cruise from that point to Harrisville. The beauty and wildness of the Oswego River on this journey through the Wharton State Forest cannot be matched in many of the wilderness areas of America.

No camping facilities are presently available in that part of Penn State Forest around the lake but camping is permitted in the undeveloped areas on either shore below the lake and in the extensive state camp below, in the Wharton State Forest, at the foot of Harrisville Lake. Such overnight camping is of course "wilderness" camping, that is to say there are few if any of the facilities available in the more developed state parks and forests. Permits may be obtained from the local ranger or at Bass River State Park headquarters.

If, instead of a day on the lake, you prefer a cruise down the river, arrange with a rental service to carry you and the canoe to the starting place, below the lake, and later have them meet you and pick up the canoe at the end of the day. If you use your own canoe, arrange if possible to have another couple go along so that one car may be left at the start, the other at the finish. Thus you have transportation back to the starting point to get the other car.

If you are fortunate enough to have one of the usual fine spring or fall days, you will breathe clean air for a change and see the unbelievable wildness and beauty of the river and the wildflowers, said to include at least twenty-five species not found anywhere else on earth. At the end of a day on the stream you will regretfully leave the river for the journey home.

If there is any doubt in your mind about the necessity of preserving this great heritage, the Pine Barrens, we suggest a careful reading of an interesting and informative booklet that may be obtained without charge from the Bureau of Parks in Trenton or at any state park in New Jersey. It is entitled *The Pine Barrens in New Jersey.*

Most canoeing groups make the run from the lake to Harrisville in half a day and do not camp en route. Others, particularly groups of Scouts, both boy and girl, and some outing clubs do camp on the sandy shores half-way down the river.

Fire permits are necessary in this area except where an

Ready to resume the cruise after lunch on a sandy shore of the river, midway to Harrisville Lake

While they are not numbered among the rare wild flowers and water plants of the Pine Barrens the fiddle head ferns grow in profusion along the Oswego. During early May these intriguing plants appear exactly like the head of a fiddle

approved fireplace is available. Rather than risk an uncontrolled brush fire we cook our meals on a single burner gasoline stove and dispense with evening campfires.

About half-way down the river there is a dam that appears to be a man-made concrete structure. It isn't, however. It is actually a dam, all the way across the stream, that is composed of the hard core of a deposit of bog iron that used to be mined in the vicinity, before the discovery of the harder ores of Pennsylvania. It is the only such natural dam we know of. Several prominent geologists, with whom we have discussed this, agree that it must be a natural dam. There was no reason for ever building a dam in that area, even during the

A typical wild and beautiful view of the Oswego halfway downstream from the lake to Harrisville. Heavy stands of aromatic southern white cedars line the shores

days of bog-iron smelting. If any of our readers has any information to the contrary we would be glad to hear of it.

The forests of Southern Atlantic White Cedar, with the sharp treetops outlined against the sky, the amber colored sweet water, photo opportunities seldom available elsewhere, and the thrill of seeing an osprey frantically trying to gain altitude as you paddle around a bend, are all sights and experiences you will long remember. Incidentally, the New Jersey Department of Forestry claims that the cedars in this area are unequalled in size and quantity anywhere else in northeastern America.

The tree roots, where they are above the surface of the swamp water and moist ground, are covered with sphagnum moss. The dense shade of the forested areas provides an ideal environment for rare ferns and other shade-tolerant wild-flowers.

Due to the fact that all of Lake Oswego and the river are wholly within the Penn and Wharton State Forests they will, we hope, remain forever in their wild state.

In our opinion, unless we, every one of us, begin to do more about our environmental spoilage than just talk, view with alarm, and hold rallies, it is very likely that one day, not too far into the future, the Pine Barrens *may* be the only area in New Jersey where we shall be able to breathe *clean* air and see *clean* water and unspoiled wilderness.

The Oswego is becoming more popular each year with outing and canoe club groups and, of course, Scout groups.

Ruins of the paper mill on the river at Harrisville. The mill was at one time the center of a prosperous community and like so many of the Pine Barrens enterprises died as a result of technological progress. The walls of the mill were of stone three feet thick

While it is doubtless a fact that more and more people enjoy the wilderness cruise down the river it never seems crowded as the many bends and the forests crowding down closely to the water quickly lose one group as another takes off and thus, while there may be a hundred canoes on the river at the same time, they are strung out for several miles.

It may seem strange that in this very populous state, should one wreck a canoe on the upper part of this river, it would be difficult if not impossible to get through the tangled swamp and forest to a highway. There is little chance of such an event, however, in this day of the sturdy aluminum and plastic canoes, but an upset can occur if one doesn't carefully watch for the logs and roots. Such a spill could be unfortunate, as it was to a couple recently who did turn over in the water on a cold October day. The dunking they got was not only uncomfortable, but the upset cost them a hundred dollars to replace a special camera lens they lost.

The most enjoyable and comfortable times to cruise in this area are during May and June and late September and October. At other times it is usually cold and raw or too hot and buggy to be thoroughly enjoyed.

The Batsto

When the Lenni Lenape lived along the shores of this quiet-flowing stream they must have loved the solitude of the vast wilderness, crossed only by their footpaths and the game trails. Today that same forest area, now a part of the Wharton State Forest, is almost as wild, with none but the usually impassable sand roads giving access to most of it.

That we have the privilege of enjoying this wilderness and its rivers by canoe, as the Indians did centuries ago, is due to the foresight of the state legislature in purchasing the area and creating the Wharton State Forest in 1954. The one hundred thousand acres, approximately one hundred and fifty square miles, comprising about 2 per cent of the total land area of the state, is a priceless heritage and the belief, held by many, that it will be preserved in its present wild state forever may turn out to be an illusion. Vested interests may one day succeed in obtaining concessions that will eventually destroy the wilderness of the Wharton Tract as they have destroyed other wild areas of the country.

The origin of the name Batsto or Batstu is said to be from the Indian, meaning "place to bathe."

Today, as one paddles or drifts in a canoe from Lower Forge or Quaker Bridge the timbers of the former bridge at Lower Forge and the present bridge at Quaker Bridge, are the only evidences of civilization encountered on the journey. It is quiet and peaceful and the hushed loveliness of sky, water, and woods offers a good tonic for the tensions

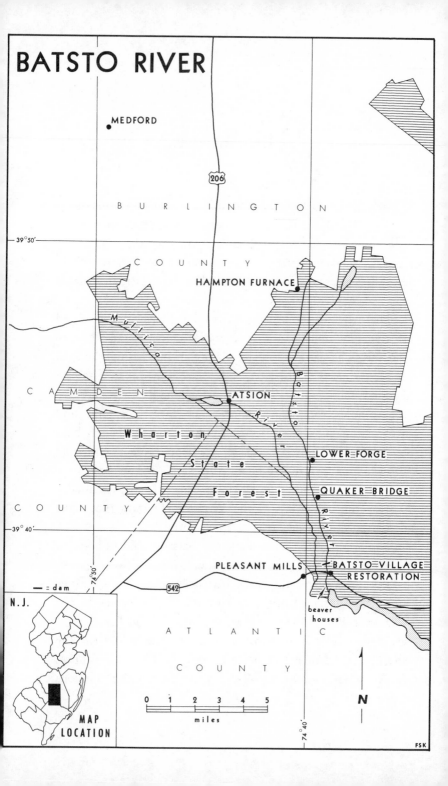

BATSTO RIVER

MEDFORD

206

B U R L I N G T O N

39°50′

C O U N T Y

HAMPTON FURNACE

Mullica

C A M D E N   C O U N T Y

ATSION

Wharton

River

Batsto

State

LOWER FORGE

Forest

QUAKER BRIDGE

C O U N T Y

River

39°40′

74°50′

PLEASANT MILLS

BATSTO VILLAGE
RESTORATION

— = dam

542

beaver
houses

N.J.

A T L A N T I C

MAP
LOCATION

C O U N T Y

0 1 2 3 4 5
miles

74°40′

N

FSK

View of the river looking downstream from the bridge on Highway 542 at Batsto. The Batsto enters the Mullica River a short distance below this point

This view above the remains of the old dam at Lower Forge is typical of
the wild upper part of the Batsto

of the modern world and we prescribe it in large doses for those so afflicted.

This stream is not one for casual afternoon paddling. It is truly a wilderness river where, if anything happened to your canoe, the only way out is on foot over the sand roads if you can find one. We consider it and the Mullica the two least accessible rivers in New Jersey and therefore the most enjoyable for cruising.

Like many of the Pine Barrens rivers the source of the Batsto is difficult to find. Its beginning is apparently a swamp pond north of the Carranza Road, three miles southeast of Tabernacle in Burlington County. It flows in a south-easterly direction through Hampton Furnace, Lower Forge, Quaker Bridge, and Batsto to the Mullica River, in which it empties a short distance below Pleasant Mills.

While it is possible to begin a canoe journey at Hampton Furnace it is not recommended because of the difficulties of access. A better starting point is Lower Forge a few miles below.

On a recent cruise from Lower Forge to Batsto we found it difficult to negotiate the five miles over the water holes on the sand road from Atsion to our starting place. However, once we were afloat below the remains of the old bridge on this unbelievably beautiful river with the blue sky overhead, filled with cottony clouds and with perfect temperature for paddling, we soon forgot such difficulties.

After taking some photographs we swung out into the fast-moving current and were on our way to Quaker Bridge, our planned lunch stop. We did not hurry and at times just drifted along with the current, thinking how fortunate we were to be able to enjoy such a beautiful day on the river.

One of the greatest pleasures of paddling on a cedar water stream in the Pine Barrens, on a warm summer day, is the delightful odor of the white cedars that fills the air.

We soon arrived at Quaker Bridge and beached our canoe for a look around. We wanted particularly to find, if possible, the remains of the nineteenth-century Thompson's Tavern that was a favorite stopping place for the patrons of the old Philadelphia to Tuckerton Stage Line that operated during the last century. We failed to find even the foundation stones nor did we see any other traces of the occupancy of the place.

Quaker Bridge might have been a large and important community had the plans for a railroad that was granted a charter in 1836 matured. However, the plans failed and so the hope for the future of Quaker Bridge also died.

As we browsed around we recalled the story of how the place received its name. It seemed that Quakers from a wide area of the countryside used to walk overland to the place

This swamp pond and drowned forest is the beginning of the principal source of the Batsto River. It is on the Carranza Road southeast of Tabernacle in Burlington County

The beginning of the sand road along the Batsto as it appears near Highway 206. To get to Lower Forge, where many canoe trips begin, calls for a drive of five miles over this sand road full of water-filled sinks and it is risky to try it with any but four-wheel-drive vehicles

of their annual meeting. They had to cross the Batsto on the way and there was no ford. People and horses had to swim, the horses carrying the old people and the children. Over the years several drownings occurred and, as a result, in 1772, the first bridge was built and it was logically named Quaker Bridge.

Early in the nineteenth century the rare curly grass fern was first discovered in the vicinity, a discovery that won international acclaim at the time. We tried, during our lunch stop, to find some of the rare plant but could not. Later on through the courtesy of Miss Ann Carter of Batsto Village we were shown a clump of the fern on the shore of a nearby bog. According to Miss Carter it is found usually under a

Throughout the Pine Barrens are seen one-time cranberry bogs like this one on the sand road between Atsion and Lower Forge. The concrete in the foreground supported the water-control gate. Once abandoned, the cranberry bogs quickly revert to their natural state

white cedar tree near water and seldom grows to a height of more than two inches.

Along the shores of the Batsto from Quaker Bridge downstream many of the unusual wild plants like the golden spike, turkey beard, fringeless orchid and many others may be seen in season.

Having lunched we shoved off again and soon encountered some heavy brush and small cedars blocking our passage. With our guide saw and hand axe we soon cleared it away. The sky remained clear and the temperature rose a bit making us somewhat sleepy from the soporific effects of the warm sun reflected from the water and the strong fragrance of cedar.

In midafternoon we arrived at the dam at the lower end of that part of the river that is known locally as Batsto Pond, where we left our canoe for a visit to the nearby historic Batsto Village Restoration.

Batsto Village was established as a bog-iron producing operation in 1766 and during the height of its production was one of the most important of all such enterprises throughout the Barrens.

During the Revolutionary War, when the British tried to sail up the Mullica River to burn the Batsto Works, they encountered such resistance from the fleet of American privateers in the river at Chestnut Neck and from the Minute Men on the shore, they gave up the attempt and retreated to the ocean and resumed their blockade of the lower river.

Quaker Bridge that crosses the river about midway between Hampton Gate and Batsto. It was on the route of an early stage run across the state to Tuckerton on the coast

The Richards mansion was the home of Colonel William Richards, the manager of the Batsto Iron Works. It is now a part of the restored historic village of Batsto and is open to the public

One of the most interesting of the many buildings in the restored village of Batsto is the general store. It is furnished as during the busy days of the bog-iron activities and many of the artifacts displayed are strange to the younger generation

As a result of the successful defense of this iron works in the battle of Chestnut Neck, the Batsto Works continued to supply the American Army with cannon balls to the end of the war. Because of the British blockade of the Mullica River the ammunition was carried overland to Valley Forge and other points.

Abandoned for almost a century, the Batsto Works seemed destined for oblivion but some years ago the Division of State Parks, Forestry and Recreation, began the extensive restoration that is now almost completed. Thousands of people from all over the country annually visit this historic village and it

A bog-iron barge, at least 150 years old, recently excavated from the mud in a nearby stream, is now on view in the restored village. It was used to carry ore to the Batsto Furnace

Iron ore from a nearby bog, on exhibit at the restoration at Colonial Batsto

Downstream about a half mile below Route 542 in Batsto, two unusually large beaver houses have been built on the shores of the river instead of in the water as they frequently are

is well worth the time and effort for anyone interested in the days of the iron empire of the Pine Barrens.

Several writers and historians have expressed the belief that restored Batsto Village is the nearest thing in New Jersey to Colonial Williamsburg in Virginia.

Returning to our canoe and making the carry around the high dam at the foot of the pond and over the low concrete dam below Highway 542, we resumed our journey. As we paddled around a bend we saw a large stick beaver house on the right shore and just below another on the other bank. Nearby we saw an oak tree ten inches in diameter which the beavers had cut through and attempted to drop across the river. They had not succeeded, as the tree caught in the crotch of another tree on the way down.

There were two things that were unusual about those

An example of the cutting power of a beaver's teeth may be seen a short distance below Highway 542 on the Batsto River. The tree which the beaver cut through is ten inches in diameter. The work of the beaver that cut the tree down was useless as in falling it was caught in the branches of another tree

beaver works: beaver houses are usually *built in water* and not on land and beavers do not, as a rule, work on hardwoods like oak. They prefer the soft woods like poplar.

After photographing the beaver works we continued to the mouth of the river and on downstream through the Mullica to the Mullica River Marina where our car had been left.

The Manasquan River
and Inlet

The Manasquan River was not included as a chapter in the earlier editions of this book because it was so full of trees and brush that canoeing on any but a small section here and there was impossible.

In 1969, under the leadership of the members of the Murray Hill Canoe Club, the Wall Township and Manasquan Kiwanis Clubs, Boy Scout Post 197, and Mr. James Truncer, superintendent of the Monmouth County Park System, several weekends were spent clearing the river from Ardena down. It was a terrific job as trees with a diameter of two feet had to be cut and hauled out of the river.

The Manasquan, despite the clearing job, is likely to be badly blocked again after each spring or fall flood. The reason for this situation is the soft loam of the banks that is easily washed from under the tree roots, causing the trees to drop into the river. In view of this, anyone planning to cruise the river would do well to look it over at each highway bridge and try to determine how bad the situation might be. However, if plans now on the drawing boards of the Division of Water Policy and Supply are approved and the necessary appropriation is voted, the Manasquan will offer excellent canoeing and fishing. The plans now under consideration call for the building of a dam and dikes above Hospital Road to create a holding reservoir which will extend upstream beyond Allaire Park with dikes to prevent flooding of that popular restoration; a pipeline extending along the shore

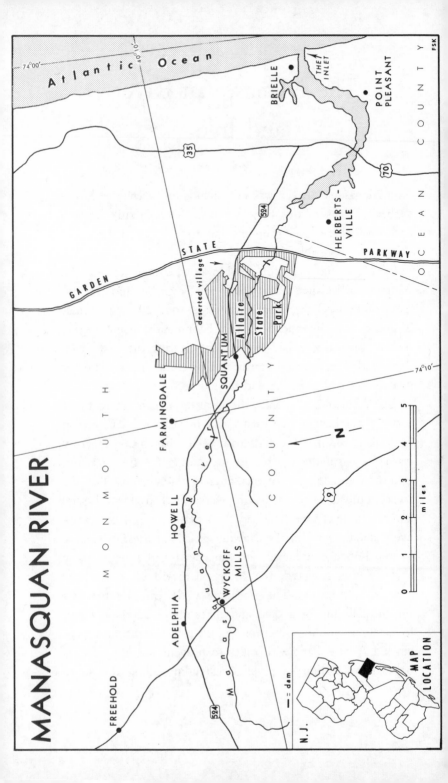

MANASQUAN RIVER

Atlantic Ocean

74°00'

40°10'

74°10'

STATE

GARDEN

PARKWAY

35

524

70

BRIELLE

THE INLET

POINT PLEASANT

HERBERTS-VILLE

deserted village

SQUANTUM

Allaire State Park

FARMINGDALE

HOWELL

ADELPHIA

FREEHOLD

WYCKOFF MILLS

Manasquan River

524

9

N

MONMOUTH COUNTY

OCEAN COUNTY

= dam

0 1 2 3 4 5
miles

MAP LOCATION

N.J.

FSK

The Howell Furnace in Allaire State Park is the only one of the bog iron furnaces left intact. It was in operation until 1848

The Manasquan River flows through Allaire Park. This view is typical of the river as it is seen from the "Red" Nature Trail in the center of the Park

upriver to the planned Manasquan River Reservoir into which water will be pumped from the lower holding reservoir. From the larger upstream facility water will be released, as needed, to maintain the proper volume and flow throughout the river below. When this work is completed the problem of falling trees and brush will no longer hinder free passage through the water to the Inlet.

In the meantime, we suggest starting trips below the concrete bridge on Route 547 which involves only a couple of hours' paddling to Allaire Park. As far as we know there is no objection to canoeists stopping at the park for picnicking and enjoyment of that very interesting restoration of a typical bog iron operation, including the Deserted Village.

To continue the river journey it is only an hour's paddle, depending upon conditions from Allaire Park to Hospital Road (the three iron arch bridge).

It should be apparent from the above that this is not one of the typical Jersey rivers that permits uninterrupted paddling for a full day. However, that is possible if such journeys include the Inlet through salt water as far as Brielle, on Route 70. Unless one is waterwise enough to anticipate sudden squalls and high seas, it is best not to try it.

However, under normal conditions of a calm day without a head wind the journey through the Inlet as far as Brielle, or for that matter to the sea at Point Pleasant, can be delightful.

For those not too interested in canoeing and particularly through the obstacle course of the down timber, we suggest

View from below the iron arch bridge at Hospital Road. The dam for the holding reservoir will be built above the bridge. When completed the reservoir will extend upstream to Allaire Park and provide deeper, debris-free canoeing water

exploring the river by car, camping overnight and spending several hours in the park. There are many roads crossing the river so that a general impression of it may be gained and the drive down along Route 524 to Manasquan and the shore is a delightful way to spend a day or a weekend. The booklet on Allaire Park which may be obtained free at the park is very informative and will help plan your journey of exploration on or along the river.

We well remember our first visit to the then Deserted Village, many years before it was restored as one of the most interesting of New Jersey's State Parks. During that visit, before the restoration in 1959 by the Division of Parks, Forestry and Recreation, the ruins of the village were somewhat spooky and mysterious. It reminded us of some of the

The restored General Store that was the company store during the heyday of Allaire. It now carries a fascinating array of merchandise

The restored carpenter shop at Allaire Park. Craftsmen now demonstrate for visitors the fashioning of various wood items that are for sale in the shop

western ghost towns we have visited. The several buildings still standing had that forlorn air common to such places. The little church, the smithy, country store and the old Post Office all were reminders of the once prosperous mill village.

As we sat on the shore of the Manasquan River that flowed past the village we tried to visualize what it must have been like in its heyday. At the height of the bog iron operations over five hundred people were employed here and the peak of iron production was between the years 1834 and 1837. From all accounts the workers were well housed in pleasant company houses, used the facilities of the large company store, and lived a generally happy life.

As with most of the little rivers of New Jersey, there are many tales about them. This one, for example, is about

The village Post Office in Allaire State Park in which the hostess, in period costume, greets visitors

The mill pond in Allaire State Park that supplied water for turning the wheels of the grist mill and other works in the iron village

The boat marina and a view of the Inlet to the north from Highway 70. The irregular shoreline of the Inlet provides pleasant canoeing waters when the weather is calm

the Manasquan. It seems that one day a group of men were working at the salt works on the shore of the Inlet and they were besieged by hungry mosquitoes. In desperation the workers crawled under a large iron kettle to escape the pests. The mosquitoes immediately began drilling through the kettle and, as each proboscis appeared on the inside of the kettle, the workmen would strike it with their hammers, riveting it fast. Finally when a number had been hammered to the inside of the kettle, the mosquitoes flew off with it after which the remainder of the swarm made short work of the men.

We like the yarn but hasten to point out as good Jerseyans that things like that happened only before the establishment of the New Jersey State and County Mosquito Control Commissions.

Another bit of folklore adds to the charm of the area. The tribes of the Lenni Lenape used to make annual pilgrimages to the shore at Point Pleasant to feast on shellfish. They came from as far away as Minisink Island on the upper Delaware River. It was in connection with those affairs that the Indians named the river and Inlet. They called it Manatahasquahan, meaning the place where they left their squaws while the male members of the tribes gathered the shellfish. They loved this river and inlet and paddled their canoes on it as we do today.

Each year in August, the people of Point Pleasant hold a community celebration to mark those early journeys to their seaside town. To the Indians Point Pleasant was a favorite place by the sea as it is for millions of annual visitors today.

The Hackensack

Known to the Lenni-Lenape Indians as "the river of many bends," the Hackensack is really a bistate stream. Its source is in Rockland County, New York.

Flowing south, it feeds the upper end of Tappan Lake, a reservoir which is also partly in the state of New York. The lake and Oradell Reservoir, farther downriver, are the main sources of water for the valley communities. The lower few miles of the river are tidal waters. That, together with the prohibition of boating on the reservoirs, limits the amount of Hackensack waters open to canoeists. However, canoeists may use several miles of the river below Tappan Lake and of course the lower reaches of the tidal water during periods of high water slack. Before launching your canoe, it would be a good idea to inquire locally whether canoeing is allowed.

As far back as the early years of the century a plan to build a dam in the vicinity of Teaneck to stop tidal flow in the Hackensack above that point, was seriously considered. Like many such plans there was a great deal of talk (as there is today about pollution problems) and the plans were forgotten. They were revived about 1935 and were again discussed at some length, and again tabled.

Possibly, out of the current agitation about water pollution and with greater money grants available, that idea or something like it may be reconsidered and the one-time clean river may be restored to its former loveliness.

In the meantime we were very much interested to read in

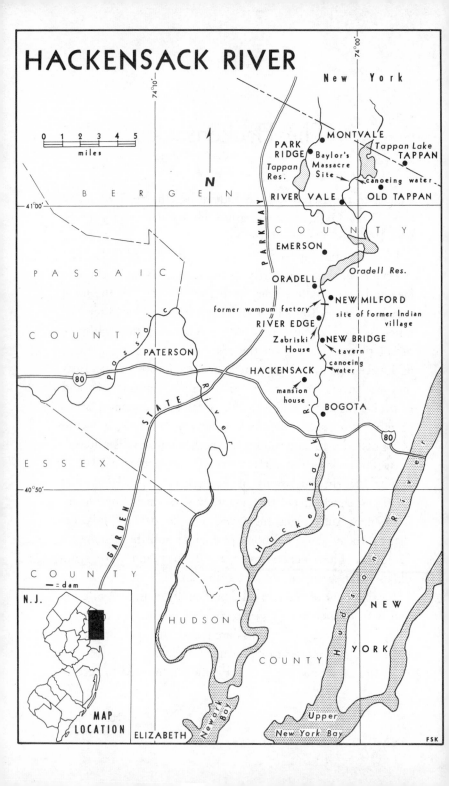

HACKENSACK RIVER

New York

74°00'

BERGEN

74°10'

PARK
RIDGE
Tappan
Res.

MONTVALE

Baylor's
Massacre
Site

Tappan Lake
TAPPAN

canoeing water

RIVER VALE

OLD TAPPAN

41°00'

COUNTY

N

EMERSON

Oradell Res.

ORADELL

PASSAIC

former wampum factory

NEW MILFORD

site of former Indian
village

RIVER EDGE

Zabriski
House

NEW BRIDGE

tavern

COUNTY

PATERSON

canoeing
water

80

HACKENSACK

mansion
house

BOGOTA

80

ESSEX

40°50'

GARDEN

STATE

River

Passaic

Hackensack R.

Hudson River

COUNTY

dam

N.J.

HUDSON

NEW

YORK

COUNTY

MAP
LOCATION

ELIZABETH

Newark Bay

Upper
New York Bay

FSK

0 1 2 3 4 5
miles

The river from the old iron bridge in River Edge, at high tide

This typical early Dutch house on DeWolf Road in Old Tappan is believed to have been built in 1704 by Cosyn Haring. It has been continuously occupied by descendants of the original owner

a recent issue of *Life* magazine, about a river clean-up job that was done by local Girl Scouts and other civic-minded people living along the river. Over a period of four Saturdays those determined conservationists actually lifted and hauled away over sixty truckloads of debris, including washing machines, steel drums, refrigerators, and even whole auto engines. The difference in the appearance of the lower river is noticeable as one drives along the river road.

Perhaps it is wishful thinking on our part and of others who remember the Hackensack, many, many years ago, but we should like to see that river again full of canoes and other small craft.

Some years ago, as we were paddling above Hackensack, we were hailed by a lady on the shore. She told us she lived nearby and seeing us swing by in our canoe reminded her of an earlier day. With a sparkle in her eye she told us about the old Kinderkamack Canoe Club that was organized by friends of hers and of the good times they used to have at their clubhouse above Oradell. As she expressed it, "Our object was to have good times together and to enjoy canoeing. We had steak and fish dinners at the clubhouse once each month." We told her we could well understand what she meant as we were also active in the American Canoe Association and our local canoe club at Bound Brook.

Our new acquaintance also told us that during those earlier

The river at the River Vale-Old Tappan line. Surrounded by busy highways and homes, it nevertheless appears like a stream in a less populated part of the State and it is on this part of the stream that canoeing is possible

This early Dutch sandstone house, on the shore of the river at River Edge, was built during the middle years of the eighteenth century by John Zabriskie. During the Revolutionary War Zabriskie became a Tory and his house was confiscated. Following the war it was presented to Baron von Steuben in appreciation of his services to the Continental Army as drill-master. It is now a museum open to the public daily for a small fee

days, when the river was clean, they used to launch their canoes at their back yard and paddle up to the club in the evening, returning to their homes late at night.

Although the Hackensack River may not offer as much canoeing water as many other New Jersey rivers, one may still find many miles on which a canoe may be used. The valley through which the river flows is rich in history, particularly of the colonial and Revolutionary War period. Its early settlers were Dutch and some of their sandstone houses, many of which were built during the early years of the seventeenth century, are still standing. One of the most notable of the early Dutch homes is the Zabriskie house in River Edge which was built early in the eighteenth century. Its builder, John Zabriskie, was an active Tory and during the Revolution his home was confiscated by the Government. After the War it was presented to Baron von Steuben, the drillmaster of the Continental Army, in recognition of his services. It is now a museum, open to the public for a small fee.

During colonial times the main road through the valley

A group of Indians in front of their bark Long House, erected on the shore of the river several years ago. Here ceremonial dances and craft demonstrations were held all summer

The site of recent excavations that uncovered several of the remains of Baylor's Dragoons who were killed in the "Baylor's Massacre" in 1778. The site is on the river in Old Tappan and the bodies were found in several tannery vats near the water

was the Old Tappan Road that followed the river to and into New York State. Today it is known variously as River Street, Kinderkamack Road, and Tappan Road.

Several years ago, while paddling near New Milford, we heard of a project that was being constructed on the river near there. We were told that two public-spirited citizens, Mrs. Vivienne Paul and her father Parselles Cole, had planned to have a replica of a Lenni-Lenape village built on the east shore of the river. A group of full-blooded Indians were brought over from Long Island, where a colony of them still live and were to erect an authentic Indian village with a bark Long House, tepees, and other structures. It was the intention of the sponsors to hold lectures, craft exhibits of artifacts to be made at the site by the Indians, and a series of motion pictures for distribution to schools throughout the State.

Despite our keen anticipation, as we resumed paddling downstream to see the progress being made, we were startled to see, as we paddled around a bend in the river, an Indian launching a birch-bark canoe. Going ashore we found the village fairly completed and many Indians in full costume. After a lot of conversation and photography we continued on our way. Last year, as we were driving along the river road

The millstone used to crush bark for the tannery operations at what later was to be the site of the "Baylor Massacre" on the shore of the river at Old Tappan. It was moved to its present location in front of the Holdrum School in River Vale and presented to the school by members of the class of 1956

we were sorry to see that no trace of that village remained.

In 1778, during the Revolution, a force of over a hundred dragoons of the Continental Army, commanded by Colonel George Baylor, were surprised in their bivouac on the bank of the Hackensack by a much larger force of British who wiped out over half of Baylor's command. The engagement has since been referred to by historians as the Baylor Massacre. Comparatively few, except students of history, remembered much of that event until a dramatic discovery of the actual site of the "massacre" was made in 1969.

In a very well-written and illustrated booklet published by the Department of Parks of Bergen County the details of the discovery and subsequent excavation are dramatically told.

The Hackensack below the lower end of the Oradell Reservoir

The salt-marsh grass that covers the "Jersey Meadows" along the Hackensack estuary may be seen waving in the breeze on any salt marsh along the shores of the rivers and bays

Thomas Demarest of Old Tappan informed Chairman Mazur of the Parks Department that he knew where the engagement had occurred and suggested that building construction be stopped in the vicinity until an excavation could be made. The details of how that important search finally disclosed the mass graves of the dragoons is well documented in the booklet which is entitled "1778 The Massacre of Baylor's Dragoons." We were given a copy of the booklet by Mr. Mazur and possibly other seriously interested people may be able to secure a copy by writing to Mr. D. Bennett Mazur, Board of Chosen Freeholders, Bergen County, Hackensack, N.J.

Little has been written about one of the most interesting phases of the Hackensack Valley history that was centered in what is now Park Ridge, known in colonial days as Pasack. For many years wampum was manufactured by the Campbell Brothers in a small factory in Pasack and traded to the Indians at the John Astor Trading Post nearby. The Post, originally a blockhouse during the Indian Wars and later, during the Revolution, a fort, was the trading post. It was there that members of the Astor family began trading wampum for furs and from that small beginning enlarged their operations in their huge northwestern fur empire.

Driving along the river today, knowing of the many evidences of our past to be seen and enjoyed in the Hackensack Valley one should, as the New York-New Jersey line is reached on the Old Tappan Road, continue into New York just a short distance and complete the day of history in the town of Tappan. It was there that the British spy, Major John André, was tried in the old Dutch church and on the hill, a short distance off Old Tappan Road, was hanged. A simple monument marks the site of his execution.

The Delaware and Raritan
Canal

In this day of tremendous mechanical earth-moving equipment, the job of digging a ditch forty-four miles long, eight feet deep, and seventy-five feet wide would not offer a serious challenge to an engineering firm. Imagine if you can, doing such a job without the aid of any mechanical equipment—just pick and shovel, wheel barrow, and horse-drawn scrapers. It seems impossible, but that was how the Delaware and Raritan Canal was built one hundred and thirty-seven years ago.

Hundreds of Irish immigrants who put their strong backs into that big job lie buried along its banks. They were victims of a cholera epidemic, and their only monument was the successful accomplishment of their great task.

The great engineering feat of building the Delaware and Raritan Canal was completed and opened for business in the summer of 1834, and for a hundred years it was a very busy and important part of the transportation facilities of that time. During the years of its active commercial use, hundreds of mule-drawn barges, and, in the spring and fall, elegant yachts, made their leisurely way through this waterway. It was a boon to the pleasure-craft owners, as it provided a quicker and safer journey to and from Florida. The sound of the tin fish horns, blowing for the locks and bridges, are heard no more. Now only canoes and other nonmotorized craft use the canal.

The Delaware and Raritan Canal, like others built during the early years of the nineteenth century, was a result of

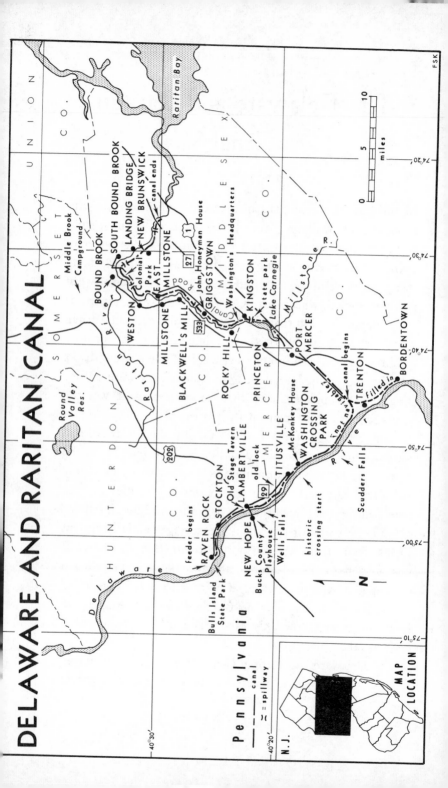

The swing bridges on the Canal and feeder have been replaced with heavier structures to carry modern traffic. Although the new structures cannot be swung open they have been designed to retain much of the charm of the older bridges

This old swing bridge at Port Mercer on the Quaker Bridge Road and others like it have been replaced with stronger wooden bridges to carry modern traffic

the ever-increasing desire for better and faster transportation of goods. The earlier stage roads were overburdened with traffic, and the canal helped relieve that situation. Most of the heavy tonnage carried between Philadelphia and New York was shipped by sailing vessels over the open sea. Due to weather conditions and lack of fair sailing breezes, it sometimes required as long as two weeks for the voyage. With the opening of the canal a safe, all-weather route was available that required only two or three days. Through the lower reaches of the Raritan River and then the canal from New Brunswick to Bordentown on the Delaware River, the barges could operate twenty-four hours a day.

Few people realize that in its heyday our canal carried a greater tonnage than did the more famous Erie Canal in New

York State. At its peak in 1859, the Delaware and Raritan handled over two and one-half million tons of cargo. Naturally this big volume of business benefited all the towns along the route. It was a great factor in the development of the economy of the entire state of New Jersey and of the ports of New York and Philadelphia.

To insure a plentiful supply of water by gravity, a dam was built across the Delaware River at Raven Rock. This provided a never-failing supply of water for the entire canal, fed through the feeder from its source to Trenton. The feeder was also used to carry coal from the Pennsylvania mines to the New York and Philadelphia areas.

All commercial activity ceased in 1932, just about a hundred

Marker beside the tracks of the Penn Central Railroad near Bordentown

years after the canal was opened to traffic. It is now owned by the state of New Jersey and is maintained by the Bureau of Water Supply in the Department of Conservation and Economic Development, as a source of potable and industrial water.

In time the feeder and the canal, now some sixty miles or more in length, will be fully developed for recreational uses. When fully utilized for these purposes its importance will be greater than at any time in its history.

The modern water-flow control gates like this one on the feeder are not as interesting as the locks were but they are more useful for the present purpose of the waterway

The canal feeder at New Jersey Washington Crossing Park. This scene is typical of the twenty miles of this popular canoeing water

Today the canal offers endless opportunities for quiet cruising, away from the noise and tension of the highways. Over sixty miles of clean water in the feeder and the main canal offer one of the finest recreational waterways open to the canoeist in the entire country. For example we have, on many trips, started at Trenton and cruised for a day or two to the head of the feeder at Raven Rock. At that point we usually carry over into the Delaware River for the faster return trip by river. On both the feeder and the river there is plenty of beautiful scenery and many things of historic interest to enjoy.

The first few miles of the feeder from Trenton are uninteresting, as that part is through the residential section of the city. It is better to start your cruise a few miles above at Washington Crossing. Before embarking at that point plan to spend an hour or so in the state parks on both the New

The Mohawk Canoe Club, on the shore of the Delaware River in Stacy Park, Trenton, founded in 1903, is one of the oldest active canoe clubs in the country. The old custom of dinner, planned and cooked by a dinner committee and served to the members at each monthly meeting at the club house, still survives. Supplementing the share-holding membership are eighty members of the Mohawk Cruisers. Unfortunately, in the summer of 1970, vandals destroyed the contents of the clubhouse and burned down the building

Jersey and the Pennsylvania sides. Enjoy the quiet sense of history that you will feel as you stand at the point where Washington and his Continental Army made their river-crossing on that historic Christmas night in 1776. On the bank of the feeder see the monument to John Honeyman, reputed to have been Washington's personal spy. Across the road, and a bit above the feeder, still stands the McKonkey

House where Washington and his men were given food and hot drinks before they started the march downriver on that very cold Christmas night.

From Trenton to Raven Rock, on the feeder, the Delaware River is never far away, and as Lambertville is approached, that fact is made evident by the roar of Wells Falls. At that point a carry around the lock is necessary. Pause a bit and enjoy these remnants of an earlier day. Until a few years ago most of the old locks and sheer-leg swing bridges were intact, and during the operational years it was always a great thrill to sneak the canoe in with a barge and thus save a carry.

Most cruisers will end their first day's journey at Lambertville. Plenty of overnight accommodations are available and you will enjoy spending an evening in this historic village. For those so inclined, the Music Circus up the hill or the Bucks County Playhouse across the river offer an excellent evening's entertainment. The Lambert House, near the feeder, offers excellent meals and overnight accommodations.

From Lambertville to the end of the feeder the countryside is less built-up and more natural. The hills of the Delaware valley become more prominent on that stretch of the feeder.

At Raven Rock the canoeist has two choices: to return to Trenton by way of the feeder, or to return by the river. One point of caution should be borne in mind if the river trip is decided upon: Unless you are a fairly competent canoeist the river journey may offer some hazards, depending upon the height of the water. The experienced paddler would not of course have any difficulty. Beginner or expert, do not attempt to run Wells Falls at Lambertville. It is an easy matter to carry your canoe around the falls on the New Jersey side of the river at that point, or end the trip via the feeder.

A mile or so above Trenton is Scudders Falls and, if you

can swim, test your paddling skill there. It is a fast run of sometimes heavy water but there are no rocks to upset the canoe.

For those who may wish to enjoy a series of afternoon journeys we suggest Princeton as the starting point. The canal, Lake Carnegie which adjoins it, and the upper Millstone are all readily accessible and in fact a journey of several days may be started at that point. Cruising down Lake Carnegie, on through the Millstone River into the Raritan and on to New Brunswick, then returning to Princeton by canal, will require several days.

During the extremely hot days the shaded reaches of Stony Brook, at the head of Lake Carnegie, are enjoyable, as are the few miles of the wild, marsh-bordered areas of the upper Millstone, east of Route 1. That part of the river is teeming with all kinds of bird life and the fall foliage is beautiful. The combination of the Canal, Stony Brook, Lake Carnegie, the Millstone and Raritan Rivers, the Canal feeder, and the Delaware River provides an unsurpassed variety of canoeing opportunity. It is easy to get to any part of those waters and trips can be planned as a series of weekends or days.

Unlike the rivers, which at times may be obstructed by down trees or too shallow to navigate, the canal is always a clean, open waterway. One may stop anywhere for a refreshing swim or a quiet rest, and in fact camp anywhere along the towpath. While no official permission has been granted it is not necessary to ask it anywhere. One is expected, however, to observe the rules of good sportsmanship and do no damage and leave the campsite as he finds it.

The towpath, once kept free of trees and brush to enable the mules to tow the barges without snagging the tow lines, is now almost completely overgrown. Because of this the canal now looks more like a natural stream than an artificial waterway.

The 137-year old Steamboat Tavern that still stands beside the Canal at the foot of Alexander Street in Princeton Basin. When the Camden and Amboy Railroad was built nearby it was renamed the Railroad Tavern

Along the route of the entire canal one may still see the old stone and plaster houses where the lock- and bridge-tenders lived. Some of them still live in the old houses, but now in retirement. At Kingston, beside the lock-tender's house, still stands a little frame building that was originally the tollhouse for the canal. It played a more important role than that, however: It was one of the first commercial installations of the Morse Telegraph which had first been put into operation a few years after the canal was opened for business. It was the principal means of communication along the entire canal.

This work boat was towed from end to end of the Canal for repair work on bridges and locks and to repair leaks in the towpath caused by muskrats. Until a few years ago it was moored in the outlet level at New Brunswick

This one-time busy waterway with the towpath covered with shade trees, as it appears today from Alexander Street in Princeton Basin. The cow lilies along the right bank add a note of color when they are in full bloom in midsummer

Originally the locks were for the purpose of raising or lowering boats from one level to another. They have now been replaced by concrete spillways to keep the water levels constant.

Since its closing to commercial navigation in 1932 the canal has been operated by the New Jersey Water Resources Commission as a reservoir to supply communities and industries along its course from Trenton to New Brunswick. The Division of Parks, Forestry and Recreation administers the recreational resources such as Bull's Island Park at the head of the feeder, and the towpath improvement and maintenance for cyclists, picnickers, campers, and canoeists.

The work on improvements to the towpath was started only a short time ago but there has already been a noticeable increase in the use of the canal and its new facilities. On any

The Ten Mile Lock, west of Bound Brook, at the time of the closing of
the Canal to commercial navigation in 1932

weekend it is not unusual to see fifty or more canoes on the
canal between Millstone and Kingston.

On Saturday afternoon, June 6, 1970, we had the pleasure
of participating in two events that marked a real beginning
of public awareness of the recreational potential of this
historic waterway. On that day the new park between the
Millstone River and the canal was officially opened for use
by Joseph J. Truncer, Director of the Division of Parks,
Forestry and Recreation, followed by a few remarks about
the history of the waterway by Kenneth Q. Jennings, vice-
president of the New Jersey Canal Society. A cannon salute
by members of the Middlesex and Somerset Jersey Blues
Militia added to the impressiveness of the occasion.

On that same day, a few miles above the Kingston Park,
in the Hoagland meadow, six hundred Boy Scouts from

numerous troops of the Thomas A. Edison Council, Boy Scouts of America, held a camporee during which they inaugurated a historic trail commemorating Washington's march along this route after capturing Trenton. The new trail, to be known as the Millstone Valley Historic Trail, extends along the towpath from Kingston to the canal bridge at Weston. It will become one of a number of such historic

Cruising Girl Scout mariners from Old Greenwich, Connecticut, portaging around the Griggstown lock

An old photograph of swing gates at the outlet lock in New Brunswick. They were removed years ago and the tide from the Raritan River now ebbs and flows through the lower level of the canal

trails established around the country to foster historical awareness in Scouts who hike and camp along them. As a national trail, the Millstone Valley Historic Trail will undoubtedly attract Scout hikers from a number of nearby states.

We still remember the many canoe rendezvous of our canoeing companions from our club at Bound Brook, many years ago. Each spring, during the boat-racing season on Lake Carnegie in May, we would get together on Friday evenings and, with duffel properly packed, start cruising up the canal. Our objective was Griggstown, fourteen miles away, which we would reach very late that night. These cruises were a lot of fun, as is always the case where ten or fifteen like-minded people get together. Camp would be made on the towpath at Griggstown, and before turning in we enjoyed an hour of campfire singing and talk.

Early in the morning we embarked for Princeton and would reach our campsite around noon, or at least in time to witness such classic events as the Carnegie or Childs Cup Races on the lake. On Sunday we would cruise down the lake and through the Millstone and the Raritan, reaching our clubhouse sometime in the evening. We heartily recommend that some of our readers get together and revive those old-time affairs. You will be glad you did, and we suspect that it will become a habit.

Despite the fact that all of the old sheer-leg swing bridges have been replaced by more modern structures to carry the heavier traffic of today, and although all the old locks have been replaced by less interesting spillways, one has the feeling, when cruising the canal today, of being actually back in an earlier century. The villages like Kingston, Griggstown, and East Millstone are still quiet little oases, little affected by the tension and hurry of modern civilization. Should you ever stop overnight at Griggstown, for example, spend an hour walking around the village in the evening. Somehow, in such a place, one expects to hear the tinkle of the mule bells and to see a canal barge come around the bend.

Perhaps the best way to get to know and love the canal is to plan a series of afternoon trips on various parts of it. You will soon discover the parts you like the best and can then plan more extensive trips as you become familiar with it.

There are still, in some of the old lock- and bridge-tenders' houses and in the old homes along the canal, people who have always lived there. Around the canal, as is true of any institution that has endured for over a century, many tales have developed. Some are true and some are otherwise. One of the old stories that has always intrigued us, and it happens to be true, is about the people who lived along a certain part of the canal in Trenton. Most of the houses had high wooden fences to keep the children out of the canal. Someone had the happy inspiration of lining his fence with bottles. When the coal barges passed the canallers just could not resist heaving coal at the bottles. Thus a winter's supply of coal was obtained without cost.

One man hit upon a better idea. He chained a pet monkey to the fence and not only obtained all the coal he needed, but enough to sell to some of his neighbors as well.

Many such yarns are still told along the canal and in the villages along the way. Seek out the people who can tell them. Hearing the stories will give you a better picture of the canal and add considerably to your enjoyment of it.

Small Streams to Explore by Car

The rivers described in the preceding pages are the principal fresh-water streams of New Jersey. On most of them it is possible to paddle a canoe for a full day or longer.

There are also a great many smaller streams that may not be characterized as canoe cruising waterways, but are worth visiting because of the scenic country through which they flow and the important historic sites to be visited. In many places one may paddle a canoe on them for short distances, and when we explore them by car we carry a canoe along in case we may want to use it.

Our selection of the noncruising streams in the following pages may not include all our readers may be interested in. Further exploration will reveal many others. Any oil company map, together with the maps at the beginning of each of the chapters on the principal rivers in this volume, will serve as guides to where to start and where to end a journey.

To explore any of the rivers by car, with no intention of using a canoe, little advance planning is necessary. Depending upon the time at your disposal, just decide on where you want to go, read any of the suggested literature, go to the head or mouth of the stream and follow it along.

Stony Brook: Hunterdon, Mercer
and Somerset Counties

It is sometimes difficult to determine the actual source of a small stream like Stony Brook but we believe the source of this stream is near Woodsville, north of Route 31.

On most New Jersey rivers the actual length of the stream is generally three to four times the distance of an air line. That is why Stony Brook doesn't appear to cover much of the three counties through which it flows. Nevertheless, according to the Stony Brook-Millstone Watersheds Association, the brook, and it is little more than that, officially begins near Woodsville where three small branches meet and form the main stream. After wandering around for some twenty miles it empties into the south end of Lake Carnegie at Princeton.

For the fisherman Stony Brook offers some trout fishing on a put and take basis. That is to say, the state puts them in for opening day in April and restocks at regular intervals and hordes of fishermen fight for elbow room in the hope of taking home a fish or two.

We like Stony Brook for quite another reason: the sport of running several miles of fast water during the spring and fall freshets. It also offers a few hours' pleasant paddling under the canopy of trees upstream from Lake Carnegie on a summer afternoon.

During flood times, for those who can handle a canoe in fast and sometimes tricky water, this stream is good for a half-day trip from a start below the bridge on Route 569 to Quaker Road. If one wants to devote a whole day to such a journey it is possible to continue all the way to Lake Carnegie or beyond, through the lake.

Stony Brook at Alexander Street, a short distance above the point where
the brook enters Lake Carnegie

The eighteenth-century grist mill on the Lamington River at Pottersville. Lack of maintenance is slowly destroying this interesting landmark

Much of the stream flows through shale cliffs and wooded countryside of suburban Princeton Township but one is not too conscious of that while running the fast water.

Under flood conditions Stony Brook may test your skill with a single blade and you may get wet negotiating one of the many bends.

The Black–Lamington River:
Morris and Hunterdon Counties

On any nice summer day, particularly when it may be a bit warm, we suggest an afternoon of exploration of this highland stream that, while it bears the names of two rivers, is actually the same stream. Why this is so we have never been able to determine.

The source is south of Route 10, near Succasunna in Morris County. It flows through Hacklebarney State Park and below the park flows through what in New England is described as a "sharp valley" that receives direct sunlight only from mid-morning to midafternoon.

The fast, shallow mountain stream, together with the shade, provides natural air conditioning for the drive along the stream to Pottersville where the valley opens up somewhat.

For many years we have fished the Black as we knew it from the park to Pottersville. In recent years a private fishing club has closed all but a mile or so of the waters to public fishing. One may, however, still find some open water and excellent trout fishing on that part of the stream for a distance of a mile or so above the village.

The Black River becomes the Lamington below Pottersville and is so designated to its mouth where it empties into the North Branch of the Raritan.

The village of Lamington, down the river a bit from

Pottersville, is a quiet farm community that does have some claim to fame. In the churchyard are the graves of John Honeyman, reputed to have been George Washington's spy, and his wife.

It is evident as one drives along this stream, nearly always in sight of it, that it is for most of its course a shallow slow-moving waterway. We have never used a canoe on the Lamington though that is possible for short distances here and there. Charming little villages, old mills, and rural scenes offer many opportunities for photography and sketching.

Pequest River: Warren and Sussex Counties

This is one of the New Jersey mountain streams with one branch flowing out of Lake Tranquility, just above the line between the two counties. The longer West Branch has its source in Hunt's Pond, near Huntsburg which, flowing generally south, joins the Tranquility branch east of Jenny Jump Mountain State Forest to form the main stream.

Route 46 follows the north shore of the main river from Great Meadows to Belvidere where it empties into the Delaware River.

While some canoeists have run parts of this stream during periods of high water, we emphatically do not recommend doing so. It is primarily a trout stream, carefully managed and kept stocked by the New Jersey Fish and Game Commission. In fact, the Pequest enjoys a reputation among New Jersey, Pennsylvania, and New York State fishermen as one of the finest trout streams in the East.

The river is worth exploring by car, even though fishing is not on your program. The river and mountain views along its whole course provide a very enjoyable few hours with perhaps a stop at any of the many picnic areas for a coffee break or picnic lunch.

Crosswicks Creek: Monmouth and Burlington Counties

This is a small stream that wanders from its source near Woodstown through pleasant countryside much like that of some parts of the extreme South Jersey area. It can be followed by car easily and, if one is so inclined a few miles of canoeing may be enjoyed in the lakes above New Egypt and at Woodstown.

The origin of the name Crosswicks came from the Indian name of "Crossweeksunk," meaning a separation.

The dam at New Egypt and the one at Woodstown were built to supply a head of water to turn the gristmill wheels. Lake Oakford, above New Egypt, is very popular for boating, skating, and other recreational activities.

Below the village the creek may be followed along either shore and it will be obvious to anyone that aside from the two ponds mentioned above no attempt should be made to canoe any part of the stream. Actually, we would characterize Crosswicks Creek as an interesting historic tour of exploration with the stream as a background.

Not far from the source of the stream is a very small settlement called Cream Ridge. There are just a few old houses along the road and of course the old church. The interesting thing about this quiet little hamlet is that it was here that Abraham Lincoln's father lived and worked as a blacksmith. The shop he operated has been allowed to disintegrate and little of it is left to see. It was from here that the Lincoln family set out for the long journey to their new home in Kentucky.

Crosswicks, the village, will require a couple of hours to fully savor its quiet eighteenth-century atmosphere. The first point of interest is the Crosswicks Chesterfield Friends Meet-

The Chesterfield Friends Meeting House in Crosswicks. The oak, seventeen feet in circumference, is believed to have been a mature tree when William Penn came to America in 1682

ing House which was built in 1773. The old wagon shed and other buildings are near the meeting house on the extensive grounds. In fact, the property is so large many people mistake the grounds for a town common or village square.

Of compelling attention, particularly to the photographer and artist, is the huge Crosswicks Oak that is over seventeen feet in circumference. Its exact age is not known but it is likely that it was a mature tree when William Penn came to America in 1682.

The Meeting House was used as a hospital during the battle between the Hessians and Continentals on June 23, 1778. During that engagement several cannonballs struck the building and one of them lodged in the north wall.

After viewing the Meeting House and grounds, walk down narrow and winding Main Street. It is still the colonial eighteenth-century village street on which many of the homes and stores are originals and not part of a restoration. The buildings are small and close to the street and it is delightful to walk along and enjoy them.

Places like Crosswicks Creek that remain as a reminder of our earlier days are getting fewer year by year with every new super highway. In the case of Crosswicks we hope it will forever remain as it is, which seems likely as new and modern roads are to be found all around it and there does not seem to be any reason for building more of them.

The Metedeconk River:
Monmouth and Ocean Counties

The village of Crosswicks retains much of its original eighteenth-century charm. Main Street, a narrow colonial way with its small homes and stores, as it appears today

In the first edition of this book, the Metedeconk was featured as a cruising river with a full chapter coverage. At that time with a lot of cutting and removing debris from the narrow and twisting stream we cruised it from Jackson's Mills to the bay at Laurelton. We had little trouble negotiating the many sharp bends because we used a thirteen-foot aluminum canoe. It was doubtful even then that a much longer canoe could get through, particularly the upper reaches.

When we again explored the stream in preparation for the revised edition of 1961, conditions were such that we were doubtful about continuing to feature it as a cruising river. However, we did include it as such but warned the reader that a lot of hard work would be required to cruise it.

Within the past three years members of the Murray Hill Canoe Club began, over a series of fall weekends, what at that time seemed to be an impossible task. The Murray Hill Club members are not only very enthusiastic and energetic canoeists, they are ardent conservationists. They gave up the pleasure of enjoyable weekend cruises to try and clear the stream in order that others might enjoy it. Anyone who has worked at clearing heavy down timber and brush from a river, particularly in late fall when the water is cold, knows what it takes.

Having again checked the river by car and making attempts at canoeing, we can well understand why the club finally gave up the task. Bill Weiller, the indomitable self-starter of the club, told us, "We tried to clear that stream." In fact, to paraphrase a well-known television commercial said Bill, "We again tried a little harder," but finally gave it up as impossible. Bill concluded with the remark, so typical of the devoted canoeist and conservationist to the effect, "We hated

This bell rang out the news of independence in 1776 and on every Independence Day until the Cumberland Court House was razed in 1846. It is now displayed in the present-day Court House in Bridgeton

to lose the Metedeconk but then there are plenty of delightful rivers to cruise in our state to keep our cruising schedule
full."

The Cohansey River, Raceway and Sunset Lake:
Cumberland and Salem Counties

Tracing the course of the Cohansey on the map, from its
source near Aldine in Salem County, to its mouth where it
empties into the lower Delaware River, one would believe
that it offers many miles of good canoeing water. That is
not the case, however, as it is not much more than a brush-
choked brook, except for two small ponds and the larger
Sunset Lake.

Sunset Lake, over a mile in length, was formed by damming
the river above Bridgeton for power purposes. A power canal
or raceway parallels the river on the west side through the
delightful city park. Residents and particularly the canoeists
call the raceway "The Northwest Passage." Within the park
there is a well-stocked zoo which attracts the children, big
and little, and other recreational facilities. There is a canoe
rental house at the Franklin Drive end of the raceway. For
those who may wish to enjoy a few hours of canoeing we
suggest paddling through the raceway and around the
perimeter of the lake.

To get to the river again it is necessary to leave the city
and drive a few miles to Greenwich. However, before
leaving Bridgeton we suggest a visit to the County Court
House on Broad Street to see, in the lobby of that building,
Bridgeton's proudest possession from its historic past. It is the
New Jersey Liberty Bell, the story of which is told on the
plaque on the cabinet in which it now rests.

The bell that hangs in this belfry rang the tidings of liberty in 1776
from the cupola of Cumberland County's first brick Court House and

IN HONOR OF THE
PATRIOTS OF CUMBERLAND CO N J
WHO ON THE EVENING OF
DECEMBER 22 1774
BURNED BRITISH TEA NEAR
THIS SITE

The Tea Burners monument on the common in Greenwich, New Jersey, commemorating the burning of British tea seized from a nearby storehouse in 1774

237

on every Independence Day until the Court House was razed in 1846. The bell was purchased by subscription and was cast at Bridgewater, Mass. in 1773.

> Tablet placed by Greenwich Tea
> Burning Chapter of the Daughters
> of The American Revolution in 1923.

Those who may be interested in further exploration of the scenes of the historic past of the region, will enjoy the quiet village of Greenwich, a few miles down the river. In a fenced-off area on the main street is the Tea Burners Monument. It was erected in commemoration of the greatest event in the history of the town, on the night of November 22, 1774. Local citizens, dressed like Indians, as were the Boston Patriots on a similar occasion, seized the tea stored in a nearby building and burned it. Any old-time resident of this delightful community will gladly discuss the Tea Party with anyone who may evidence some interest.

The Cohansey at Greenwich, on the shore of which was located the building from which the tea was taken and burned, is tidal water and from there to the Delaware River a strong tide ebbs and flows. The river, like all tidal estuaries, wanders over the countryside in long loops between shores covered with marsh grass.

It is possible to paddle a canoe on this stretch of water if one is weatherwise enough to anticipate the sudden squalls and doesn't mind bucking a fast incoming tide. It is not worth while, however, not to mention the danger, as the entire river from Greenwich to the Delaware is uninteresting except to power boatmen on their journeys to the lower river and bay. It is not advisable to cruise on this part of the Cohansey in any small craft without power to get back against an adverse tide.

Cruising and Camping Equipment

We have often been asked about the outfits we use on our day or overnight canoe journeys. The photographs on the following pages show a complete, light-weight and nesting cooking outfit, our single-burner stove with wind shield that we regularly use for both cooking the midday meal for just a single day of cruising and also for cooking our meals on journeys of several days. With this outfit we can cook and serve a meal for two consisting of as many as five courses and everything hot. For example, if the meal is to consist of soup, boiled potatoes, canned peas, and fried ham or bacon and eggs, we first heat up the soup and serve it in the two aluminum bowls. Then we put the potatoes on the stove to boil. While they are cooking we eat the soup and within a few more minutes we drain and cover the potatoes to keep them hot. An alternative would be to wrap the potatoes in heavy aluminum foil and that will keep them hot for a half-hour. In a small pan we heat up the peas and when they are hot (just a few minutes) drain them and cover the cooking pot with foil or a cover if available. Then the *pièce de résistance*, the ham or bacon and eggs. When they are cooked, serve them, the potatoes and the peas, all piping hot.

While you are finishing that part of the meal the water should be on the stove, ready for instant coffee or tea with your dessert. Sound complicated? It isn't. Try it sometime and get more enjoyment from your day afloat.

Coleman stove, canoe cooking outfit, stove shield, reflector oven, and pack basket

A cooked meal is much better than a cold picnic lunch, especially on the cooler days of spring and fall.

If you use a stove, single or double burner, do not use gasoline. It is better to use the special fuel made by the Coleman Company that is available in any hardware or sporting goods store; with this fuel your stove will never foul up and spoil a day or a trip.

Shown in the photographs are also the pack basket we use, a duffel bag with our air beds and sleeping bags for overnight, and a sportsman's saw for clearing timber on some of the rivers. Also included is our pride and joy, a reflector aluminum oven which we made ourselves from a sheet of aluminum and wire from coathangers. With it placed in front of a regular camp fireplace or a backlog of stones or some other reflecting surface we make wonderful biscuits in a few minutes. Packaged Bisquick and water is all that is needed.

In the pack basket (an inexpensive plastic trash bag or two will do as well) we carry all the duffel and our camera with a rainproof cover.

So much for the light and compact canoe outfit. We also use a much more elaborate and heavier outfit for another kind of cruising. That is when we journey over a wide range in the Adirondacks or Blue Ridge Mountain country of Virginia and North Carolina. On such trips we carry the outfit in the trunk of our car with the canoe on top of the car so we may stop on the way and cruise for half a day or longer on such streams as the upper reaches of the James

The more elaborate and comfortable motor camping-canoe cruising outfit we use. The camp shown here was set up on the Appalachian Trail in North Carolina

Canoe on its side with tarpaulin rigged over it for day emergency and overnight shelter. Ample protection in any but severe storms

Demonstrating the use of canoe pole in the Great Egg Harbor River, below Penny Pot

in Virginia or on a lake that may give us good fly fishing. As this is written we are preparing for our annual two or three weeks' motor camping and canoe trip along the Blue Ridge Parkway in Virginia and North Carolina and down to the Great Smokey Mountain National Park in Tennessee.

Sooner or later, if you are going to follow the water trails, you will want to try overnight camping on canoe and motor journeys.

If you have a light-weight cruising tent, sleeping bags and air beds, the rest of an outfit is no problem. A six-by-ten-foot tarpaulin or plastic sheet can be used as an emergency shelter during the day and for protection at night. Used as shown with the canoe, such a rig will be comfortable in any but a driving rainstorm.

On some of the fast and shallow waters we pole the canoe instead of paddling it. It is an art that all canoeists should master as the standing position gives a better view ahead to pick a channel than does a kneeling position for paddling.

Let no man say,
and say it to your shame,
that all was beauty here
before you came.

PEMBERTON TOWNSHIP
RECREATION COMMISSION

Canoe Rental Directory

The following listing of places where canoes may be rented is accurate up to the time of the publication of this book. For the convenience of the reader the listings are by towns in alphabetical order, followed by the location and phone number. At some places canoes may be rented for use on other rivers if carried by the customer. At others arrangements may be made to have the canoe and passengers carried to the place of embarkation, and picked up at the take-out point. Still others will not permit the use of their canoes except on the water at which it is rented.

Prices are not included here as they vary a great deal. However, most of them are reasonable and, whether a canoe is rented for an hour, a day or longer, one would have to do a great deal of canoeing to match the cost of a new canoe. For those who may regularly use a canoe personal ownership will give more satisfaction. Depending upon the interest and whether or not extensive use of a canoe will be made, it would be better for a year or so to rent them.

It is advisable to make reservations in advance by phone or mail as it is difficult sometimes to get a canoe on a weekend or on a holiday without reservations.

ASBURY PARK
  Sunset Landing on Deal Lake
  1215 Sunset Ave.   Phone 201-776-9732

BERKELEY HEIGHTS
Explorer Post #68 B.S.A.
Frank Schade, 96 Old Farm Road   Phone 201-322-1676

BRIDGETON
Bridgeton Pleasure Boat Co.
City Park, 68 Franklin Drive   Phone 609-455-5303

CLINTON
Hunterdon Equipment and Marine
7 Old Highway 22   Phone 201-735-5832

CRANFORD
Cranford Boat and Canoe Co.
Springfield and Orange Aves.   Phone 201-272-6991
(If no answer, call 201-232-8263)

EAST MILLSTONE
Millstone Canoe Rentals
Amwell Road   Phone 201-844-9440
(Also rent Folboats and kyacks)

GREENBANK
Mullica River Boat Basin
R.D. 2, Egg Harbor   Phone 609-965-2120

Belle Haven Lake, R.D. 2, Egg Harbor
On Route 542   Phone 609-965-2031

KINGSTON
Bernard's Boat Rental
Box 229   Phone 609-924-9818

LAMBERTVILLE
Lambertville Marina
Coryell's Ferry, Box 211   Phone 215-862-5507

Golden Nugget Canoe Rental
Route 29

MAYS LANDING
Lenape Park Recreation Center
Park Road R.D. 2, Weymouth   Phone 609-625-1191

Winding River Campground
Box 246 R.D. 2, Weymouth   Phone 609-625-3191
(On Route 559)

MILLSTONE
Mill-at-the-Forge Canoe Rental
River Road   Phone 201-359-5279

MILLVILLE
Dick's Canoe Rental
320 High St., P.O. Box 67   Phone 609-805-1000

MT. HOLLY
Hack's Canoe House
100 Mill St.   Phone 609-267-0116

Jones Canoe Rental
R.D. 1, Route 206   Phone 609-267-6871

PEMBERTON
Ben's Canoe House (at the river bridge)
Phone 609-894-8655

PHILADELPHIA
Flat Rock Dam Rental
223 Gates St.   Phone 215-483-4390

POMPTON PLAINS
Rentals Unlimited
444 Hwy. 23   Phone 201-839-1210

RAMSEY
R/U Ski and Sport
Highway 17   Phone 201-327-8102
(Also rent kyacks)

SWEETWATER
Mullica River Marina   Phone 609-561-4337
Elmer L. Keller   RFD 1, Hammonton

TITUSVILLE
Abbott's Marine Service (on Canal Feeder)
Route 29   Phone 609-737-3446

TOMS RIVER
Camp Alboconda
1480 Whitesville Road   Phone 201-349-4079

CANOE CRUISES
South Branch Canoe Cruises
R.D. 1, Lebanon   Phone 201-236-2716
Conducted cruises for groups up to 30 on rivers in New
Jersey and eastern Pennsylvania.

Suggested Reading

Exploring the little rivers by canoe is quite different from an afternoon paddle or a canoe race meet or regatta. The streams described in the foregoing pages flow through a beautiful and historic land. To enjoy them more fully we suggest some preliminary reading about the area to be explored.

So much has been written about the Pine Barrens, the old forgotten towns, the exploits of the eighteenth-century privateers and smugglers, to mention but a few of the facets of New Jersey history, that a bit of study beforehand will quicken the anticipation. One cannot help but feel a deep sense of history on a leisurely canoe or car journey through any part of New Jersey.

The following list of titles, though far from complete, will help inform the reader of places that will be enjoyed, depending on the degree of interest in such places. A few of the books are out of print (OP) but can be found in most public libraries. Titles available in paperback are so indicated (PB).

American Red Cross. *Canoeing*. New York: Doubleday & Co., 1957.
Beck, Henry Charlton. *Forgotten Towns of Southern New Jersey*. New Brunswick, N.J.: Rutgers University Press, 1961 (PB).
———. *Jersey Genesis*. New Brunswick, N.J.: Rutgers University Press, 1963 (PB).
———. *The Jersey Midlands*. New Brunswick, N.J.: Rutgers University Press, 1962 (PB).

————. *More Forgotten Towns of Southern New Jersey*. New Brunswick, N.J.: Rutgers University Press, 1963 (PB).

Boy Scouts of America. Merit Badge Pamphlet on Conoeing. New Brunswick, N.J.

Boyer, Charles S. *Early Forges and Furnaces in New Jersey*. Philadelphia: University of Pennsylvania Press, 1963.

Cawley, James S. *Historic New Jersey in Pictures*. Princeton, N.J.: Princeton University Press, 1939 (OP).

Cawley, James S. and Margaret. *Along the Delaware and Raritan Canal*. Rutherford, N.J.: Fairleigh-Dickinson University Press, 1970 (PB published by A. S. Barnes).

Leiby, Adrian C. *The Revolutionary War in the Hackensack Valley*. New Brunswick, N.J.: Rutgers University Press, 1962.

Menzies, Elizabeth G. C. *Millstone Valley*. New Brunswick, N.J.: Rutgers University Press, 1969.

Miers, Earl Schenck. *Where the Raritan Flows*. New Brunswick, N.J.: Rutgers University Press, 1964 (PB).

McPhee, John. *The Pine Barrens*. New York: Farrar, Straus & Giroux, 1968.

Pierce, Arthur D. *Family Empire in Jersey Iron*. New Brunswick, N.J.: Rutgers University Press, 1964 (PB).

————. *Iron in the Pines*. New Brunswick, N.J.: Rutgers University Press, 1957 (PB).

————. *Smugglers' Woods*. New Brunswick, N.J.: Rutgers University Press, 1960 (PB).

Rutgers University, Cooperative Extension Service, College of Agriculture and Environmental Science. *A Guide to Nature Study in New Jersey*. Leaflet 433, 1968.

Van Dyke, Henry. *Days Off and Other Digressions*. New York: Charles Scribner's Sons, 1920.

————. *Great Short Works of Henry Van Dyke*. New York: Harper & Row, 1966.

Veit, Richard F. *The Old Canals of New Jersey: A Historical Geography*. Little Falls, N.J.: New Jersey Geographical Press, 1963 (OP).

Weygandt, Cornelius. *Down Jersey*. New York: Appleton-Century, 1940 (OP).

Wildes, Harry Emerson. *Twin Rivers: The Raritan and the Passaic*. New York: Rinehart & Co., 1943 (OP).

The New Jersey Division of Parks, Forestry and Recreation has published a great deal of useful and interesting information, including an official map of the state and numerous regional maps. It may be obtained at the headquarters of any of the state parks, or by mail from the Bureau of Parks, P.O. Box 1420, Trenton, N.J. 08625. The following is a partial list of such materials:

The Pine Barrens of New Jersey
Map of the Pine Barrens
Stephens-Saxton State Park
Rates for Day Use and Overnight Facilities
State Forest and Park Campgrounds
Year Round Guide to New Jersey State Forests, Parks, Natural
   Areas and Historic Sites
Lebanon State Forest
Wharton State Forest
Washington Crossing State Park
Bass River and Penn State Forest
Belleplain State Forest
Canoeing in New Jersey

Many of the New Jersey County Park Commissions have booklets and maps of their parks and recreational facilities. They may be obtained by writing to the Park Commission at the county seat of the county in which you are interested.

ABOUT THE AUTHORS

James and Margaret Cawley are without doubt the world's most durable canoeists. They met on a canoeing party; they were married in 1920 and for their honeymoon took a canoe camping trip. A couple of years later their daughter at the age of six months was taken on her first canoe cruise and overnight camp.

Jim was brought up with canoes, his father having joined the American Canoe Association in 1890. The family lived in Bound Brook, near the Canal, the Millstone, and the Raritan. At twelve Jim undertook to build his own canoe and the craft, made of barrel staves and salvaged boards, took him all the way to Kingston on his first overnight cruise.

Margaret Cawley was born in Brooklyn and educated as a professional musician, a piano accompanist and member of a symphony orchestra. She reverted to amateur status after her marriage and the Cawleys raised three daughters while Jim was pursuing his career in advertising sales. Meanwhile the family continued canoeing and camping. Margaret does the color photography for the slides used in the Cawley lectures on outdoor activities and regional history.

In 1942 the Cawleys published the first edition of *Exploring the Little Rivers of New Jersey*. They made a complete revision in 1961 and in 1969–70 they cruised the entire length of every stream covered in the book in preparation for the present edition. Jim, a photographer of professional caliber, took a new set of illustrations.

Jim retired in 1954 and he and Margaret have continued an active outdoor life with intervals of study, writing, collecting New Jersey artifacts, and lecturing. *Along the Old York Road* was published in 1965 and *Along the Delaware and Raritan Canal* in 1970.

One of the present preoccupations of the Cawleys is watching the progress of a fourth generation of canoeists—their seven grandchildren.